Applying
Heart-Centered
Metaphysics

A Workbook to Bring Metaphysics to Life in *Your* Life

Paul Hasselbeck

Cher Holton

unity®
Books

Unity Village, MO 64065-0001

Applying Heart-Centered Metaphysics

First edition 2012

Unity Books titles are available at special discounts for bulk purchases for study groups, book clubs, sales promotions, book signings or fundraising. To place an order, call the Unity Customer Care Department at 1-866-236-3571 or email *wholesaleaccts @unityonline.org*.

Cover design by: Karen Rizzo
Interior design by: The Covington Group

Library of Congress Control Number: 2011932741
ISBN: 978-0-87159-357-3
Canada BN 13252 0933 RT

CONTENTS

Section 4: Proving the Truth We Know

INTRODUCTION

Imagine the luxury of having a workbook of exercises at your fingertips, designed to help make the principles of metaphysics practical, easy to understand, and useful in your life. Wouldn't it be wonderful to be able to manifest the spiritual laws and principles in your life, knowing you could meet any situation you face from your highest, most elevated level of Consciousness? That concept is what prompted the creation of this book!

What Makes This Book Different?

This is a practical workbook, created to complement the textbook *Heart-Centered Metaphysics: A Deeper Look at Unity Teachings* by Paul Hasselbeck (Unity Books, 2010). It is designed to help you put metaphysical teachings into practice in a current, reality-focused way. It offers a very practical application of metaphysical teachings so you can begin applying them to your life immediately.

If you've ever wondered why metaphysical principles are sometimes so difficult to understand and apply, think about this: While discussions about metaphysical concepts and principles have probably been around since humankind began wondering about anything beyond the physical realm, these teachings have always been expressed in the language of the time. Since the advent of New Thought in the late 1800s, these concepts have been couched in the context of Newtonian or classical physics. This is a model of separate objects acting upon one another in some way, shape or form. It is a world of cause and effect. One example of how classical physics affected New Thought lies in the concept of Divine Ideas (objects of and in Consciousness) that literally exist in Divine Mind.

Understanding Our Writing Style

We made the conscious decision to use new writing conventions to enhance your ability to understand metaphysical teachings. For example, as you read you will notice we use the language of Oneness, letting go of language that implies separation. For instance, phrases such as "I am one with God" and "I am co-creator with God" have been expressed in terms emphasizing our Oneness rather than separation. "I am one with God" becomes "I am Oneness." In addition, typical writing style supports capitalizing references to the Divine or God, while not capitalizing any reference to our divinity (as this sentence demonstrates). In this text we make no such distinction, since this distinction simply reinforces a sense of separation and difference. For us, the Divine or God is the same as the Divine of us; It is the same Consciousness.

How to Use This Workbook

This workbook follows the same pattern of chapters as *Heart-Centered Metaphysics* and offers specific practices intended to enhance your understanding of the Teachings, as well as increase your ability to use them in your day-to-day life. Our goal is to move beyond simply intellectualizing these teachings and guide you in realizing Truth and using It in your everyday life. Each chapter focuses on the specific topic explored in the corresponding chapter in *Heart-Centered Metaphysics*, and is divided into the following five sections, plus the Answer Key:

Why Is This Important? We've included our comments about why this particular concept is important to you as you relate it to your spiritual growth and understanding.

What's in It for Me? This section helps you connect the dots between the metaphysical concept and its practical application in your own personal experience.

Application Examples: We've shared a few specific examples of the principle in action so you can put the concepts into a realistic, practical context.

Heart of the Matter: This is where we pass the baton to you! It's your turn to look at what you've learned in the chapter and summarize the key concepts you found most important.

Putting It Into Practice: Finally, we offer a few exercises geared toward helping you solidify your understanding of this material and see it work in your own life.

Answer Key: Don't we all wish life came with an Answer Key? Obviously, when we are talking about metaphysical principles and concepts, there is a lot of room for personal interpretation of our experiences, as well as ongoing expansion of awareness and consciousness. However, we have tried to help you in your study by providing examples of answers that are on the right track, where appropriate. This section is included at the back of the book, so you aren't tempted to just skip the work and read our ideas!

We strongly recommend the use of a personal journal in conjunction with this workbook to capture your ideas, experiences and insights as you study and practice. As you progress, you may find it helpful to review past entries in your journal to identify trends, patterns and areas where you have progressed.

This is a book to be used again and again, because we are all on our spiritual journey of growth and development. New awareness leads us to a higher understanding. Our wish is for you to become intimately connected to the Truth Principles of Heart-Centered Metaphysics as you become the best Christ you can be!

Section 1:

Foundational Principles and the Highest Form of Mind Action

CHAPTER ONE

METAPHYSICS AND TRUTH

Why Is This Important?

The Absolute Realm does not change; It is utterly dependable. Therefore we can depend on Divine Ideas, Laws and Principles with even more assurance than we do upon the seemingly unchanging natural laws of the relative realm like gravity and electricity. The relative realm changes; it can be modified, shaped and reshaped. If we do not like what we see or experience, we can change it. The choice is always ours.

What's in It for Me?

You have varying degrees of power over what you see and experience. The bottom line is—you have power! The power to change is always in your hands—and the process starts with your mind!

If you do not like what you see (your external experience), you *may* be able to change it depending on your sphere of influence.

If you do not like your internal experience, you can definitely change it. You are 100 percent responsible for your internal experiences. While you may or may not be responsible for the external events in your life, you *are* responsible for your reactions to those events. Whether recognized or not, you have power over your thoughts, feelings and actions.

Application Examples

1. You find yourself in a traffic jam. You have no power over the event—the traffic jam. However, you do have power over what you think and feel about it. If you begin to grumble about it, you intensify your feelings as you think about it more and more. (See Chapter 20 in *Heart-Centered Metaphysics* for more on Thought/Feeling and the Law of Mind Action.) Once you are aware of doing this, you are able to conclude your reactions are of the relative realm and are therefore changeable. You then decide to change your thoughts and feelings about it. (See Chapter 22 in *Heart-Centered Metaphysics* for more on Denials and Affirmations—how to change your thoughts and feelings.)

2. You are in a job you do not like. Because this is in the relative world of change, you can either search for a new job or change what you think and feel about the current job.

3. You design a garden. As you plant the garden, you can change your design to your liking as you go along. At any point in time, you can change the appearance or content of your garden.

4. No matter what you think, feel, say or do, everything—*everything*!—is based on and in Divine Ideas, Principles and Laws. You have the power to consciously choose to access your Divine Nature (God, Christ) to decide what to think, feel, say or do.

The Heart of the Matter

In five sentences or less, summarize the key ideas, the essence, of Chapter 1: Metaphysics and Truth.

_____

_____

_____

_____

_____

_____

Putting It Into Practice

- Read each statement below, and determine whether it is relative (r) or Absolute (A).

    ____ There is no death.
    ____ There is no sickness.
    ____ The economy is in the tank.
    ____ Life is not fair.
    ____ There is only Good.
    ____ Ice cream is yummy.
    ____ Chocolate makes me feel better.
    ____ There is no evil.
    ____ Life is good.
    ____ I am the Good.

- Why is it important to distinguish between the Absolute and the relative? How does knowing this make a difference in your life?

- Look at one or more situations in your life (such as paying the mortgage, juggling priorities, raising children). Become aware of your internal dialogue related to the situation(s) you selected. Are the statements relative or Absolute? If you realize your statements are relative, what Absolute statements could you replace them with to redefine or refocus your consciousness?

- As you review Chapter 1, Section D, in *Heart-Centered Metaphysics* on relative existence, reflect back on a project you have recently completed. Before you began the physical work on the project, you had thoughts and ideas about it. Make a list of possible First Cause Divine Ideas that stimulated your relative thoughts and ideas about the project (first effect, which then becomes the second cause).

LIFE IS CONSCIOUSNESS

Why Is This Important?

We must remember everything begins, exists and ends in consciousness. Somehow, somewhere, everything we think, say and do begins in consciousness. What we call our life is an experience of our consciousness. The more we become aware of what is in our consciousness and how we use it, the better able we are to take control over it. When we use our consciousness unconsciously, we tend to have more experiences we do not want ... or at least do not consciously choose. By paying attention to the quality of our experiences, we can begin to notice whether we are living in and from victim, victor, vessel or Verity consciousness.

What's in It for Me?

Just as you learned in Chapter 1, you have the power to be aware of what is happening in your own consciousness, in your own mind (not the brain!). Once you are aware, you actually choose the overall type of consciousness (personality or Individuality, error consciousness or Christ Consciousness) as well as the level of consciousness (victim, victor, vessel or Verity) from which you live, and you can decide whether to keep doing more of the same or make another choice. For example, when you notice you live in victim and error consciousness, you can decide if you like it or not. If you like it, stay with it. If you do not like your experience, then change your mind/change your consciousness. The bottom line is that you are not a victim of your own consciousness. You simply experience the effects of your thoughts and feelings. You are and have the power to change and overcome any limiting thought, idea, belief or feeling.

When you realize there is a Higher Power and, in Truth, you are It, you enter into a vast field of possibilities, potential and self-responsibility. Use this realization to motivate yourself to move as often as possible into the state of awareness of the Oneness (Divine Mind) you already are. You will then have the confidence to meet the world consciously on your own terms and not create the experience of the world dictating its terms to you.

Bottom line—lead from your Divine Nature in all things. In doing so, you can always trust that all Its abilities are always present and available. Involution (going inward in consciousness to the Divine you already are) precedes evolution (the evolution and elevation of your seemingly limited consciousness). The more you do this, the more you can authentically be the Christ, the Divine, that you already are in Truth.

Application Examples

If you have the experience of being victimized by other people, situations or even God, you can change this experience. Whether you have been fired, lost money in the stock market, been dumped by a friend or partner, or have a picnic rained out, you are actually the one deciding how you choose to experience the event. It is not forced upon you by anything external. In the English language, we often phrase our experience from a victim perspective. Other languages have victim consciousness even more embedded in them. For example, in Spanish, when a person misses the bus he/she will say something like "The bus left me!" While this is factually true, the bus actually left as scheduled, and the person was left behind because he/she was not there to get on the bus! The bus was not responsible; the person was.

Victim consciousness is often loaded with the sense that you cannot do anything about it. You feel helpless and out of control. You can feel victimized by the economy, another's actions or choices, or even the weather! You can seem to even victimize yourself through your own negative self-talk. As long as you keep empowering the victim viewpoint, you will do little or nothing about it. However, once you are aware, you can jump into action. Through and from the power of mind/consciousness, you can move to any of the other three levels of consciousness. Again, you get to choose which one!

1. **Moving from victim to victor consciousness** happens when you realize you have the power to change your mind and therefore, your experience—no matter what! It comes from the realization that your intellect has power over your mind/consciousness—over your thoughts, beliefs, feelings and actions. This is the movement from victim consciousness (thinking everything happens *to* you (including your thoughts, beliefs and feelings) to realizing you actually choose this experience via the power of your mind/consciousness. This is the realization that your experience of the world around you is happening *by* you instead of *to* you! However, in order for there to be a victor, there still must be a victim!

2. **Moving from victim or victor consciousness to vessel consciousness** happens when you realize there is a Higher Power over your intellect. This Higher Power helps you in some way. It has Power over you. This level involves the belief that everything is happening *through* you from some Higher Power/God; It happens through you, and out to the world around you. Notice, even at this level, something is happening *to* you! Notice vessel consciousness is simply a kind of "positive victim consciousness"— God/Higher Power is happening to you.

3. **Moving from victim, victor or vessel consciousness to Verity Consciousness** happens when you realize there is a Higher Power *and* It is your True Reality. You also realize you can use your True Reality to overcome and/or change your thoughts, beliefs and feelings because the Truth of you is the "vast, unformed potential" of the Oneness you already are. Your True Nature is happening *from* you—not *to* you or *through* you! It *is* you!

The Heart of the Matter

In five sentences or less, summarize the key ideas, the essence, of Chapter 2: Life Is Consciousness.

_____

_____

_____

_____

_____

_____

Putting It Into Practice

- Read each description below and determine which level of consciousness is demonstrated (victim, victor, vessel or Verity):
    - Why does my line always move slowest at the supermarket?
    - From my Oneness, I knew what to do.
    - How can I be prosperous when the economy is so bad?
    - I can overcome this situation.
    - I claim the Abundance that is mine by right of Consciousness.
    - If my parents had let me take dance lessons, I would be a dancer today.
    - It wasn't me. It was God working through me.
    - Even though I did not get to take dance lessons as a child, I can take them now.
    - Make me an instrument.
    - While this line moves slowly, I can read the funny titles in the tabloids.
    - I was called to do this.
    - I Am.

- Think of your own examples from your own experience:

    A. victim consciousness

    B. victor consciousness

    C. vessel consciousness

    D. Verity Consciousness

- Write your own short centering phrase to use whenever you notice that you are coming more from your ego or intellect.

_____

_____

- While the goal is to keep our focus always on and coming from the Oneness, sometimes it is helpful to use our senses as reminders of that Oneness:

    A. Touch—Choose a small object that you can carry with you such as a stone or bead.

    B. Sight—Choose a visual image, such as picturing your heart as a golden orb of radiating light.

    C. Smell—Choose a pleasing scent that evokes Oneness for you. For example, aromatherapists suggest that lavender produces a soothing sensation; vanilla is relaxing and comforting; and ginger reduces tension.

    D. Taste—Choose your favorite flavor (for example, citrus, peppermint, cinnamon or chocolate) to carry around in whatever form that works for you (such as a piece of candy, chewing gum, a breath lozenge).

    E. Sound—Choose a song to hum whenever you want to evoke the awareness of Oneness.

CHAPTER THREE

SELF-KNOWLEDGE

Why Is This Important?

Self-observation leads to self-awareness, which leads to self-knowledge. When we are aware of what we are thinking and feeling, we can consciously choose whether we want these thoughts and feelings ... or not. We use self-observation and self-awareness to know ourselves.

Self-awareness and self-knowledge need not be linked to guilt, self-recrimination or self-condemnation. If we feel guilty, feel self-judgmental or condemn ourselves, then we have even more to work on and change.

What's in It for Me?

You are never stuck with who you think or feel you are, nor are you stuck with who you think and feel other people are. If you do not like what you are aware of about yourself or others, you can change it. If you boldly and bravely enter into self-observation, you can truly know yourself from a place of candid self-awareness. You can face up to the good, the bad and the ugly! Then, from this place of honest self-awareness, you can change yourself—if you so choose.

Likewise, you are never stuck with who others think or feel you are. While you cannot change others' thoughts and feelings about you, you do have total control over what *you* are thinking in response to them!

Ultimately, you can use your self-awareness and self-knowledge to be the Christ you already are—more and more every day!

Application Examples

1. As in Chapter 2, let's say you find yourself in a traffic jam. You are self-aware that you are getting agitated and upset. Remember that if you begin to grumble about the situation, your feelings intensify as you continue to think about it. (See Chapter 20 in *Heart-Centered Metaphysics* for more on Thought/Feeling and the Law of Mind Action.) From your self-awareness and self-knowledge, you know you have no power over the event, the traffic jam. However, you do know you have power over what you think and feel about it. You know:

   • The traffic jam and your reaction to it are in the relative realm and changeable.

- You are currently coming from victim consciousness, and this is something you can change. Determine from what level of consciousness you prefer to respond while in the traffic jam.

- You can change your thoughts and feelings about this traffic jam. (See Chapter 22 in *Heart-Centered Metaphysics* for more on denials and affirmations and ways to change your thoughts and feelings.) You know that denials and affirmations are more examples of the Law of Mind Action. You know that this law is always in play. It is of the Absolute so you cannot change it, work around it, or ignore it.

2. You can also use your self-observation and self-knowledge to become aware that there is this inner urge to more and more be "the Good," be the Christ you already are! You use self-observation and self-awareness to know whether you are being Christ, whether you are living from the awareness of the Oneness, your Divinity, what you truly are. From here you can take action. You can use unchanging Divine Ideas and call forth the Twelve Powers into your awareness and into action. (See Chapters 24 and 25 in *Heart-Centered Metaphysics* for more on the Twelve Powers.)

3. To become more aware of your True Divine Nature, use prayer and any type of meditation that allows for the Silence to arise. (See Chapters 6, 7 and 8 in *Heart-Centered Metaphysics* for more on the Silence, Meditation and Prayer.)

The Heart of the Matter

In five sentences or less, summarize the key ideas, the essence, of Chapter 3: Self-Knowledge.

_____

_____

_____

_____

_____

Putting It Into Practice

- Make a list of what you know for sure about yourself. Also, indicate whether it is relative or Absolute and why.

_____

_____

_____

_____

_____

- Descartes famously said, "I think, therefore I am." Take a few moments and fill in the blanks with verbs you feel describe the essence of who you are.

   "I _____, therefore I am."

   "I _____, therefore I am."

   "I _____, therefore I am."

   "I _____, therefore I am."

   "I _____, therefore I am."

- Now take the list you just created and flip-flop the sentence. For example, Descartes said, "I think, therefore I am." If you flip-flopped that sentence, you would have, "I am, therefore I think." What does flip-flopping the sentences tell you about yourself from a metaphysical perspective?

CHAPTER FOUR

EVOLVING SPIRITUAL AWARENESS, BUILDING CHRIST CONSCIOUSNESS

Why Is This Important?

The more we evolve and build our awareness of what this Christ is (the Idea that is made up of Ideas), the more we can be It and live from It. The more we can be It and live from It, the more we are centered, peaceful and helpful to others. We are no longer tossed about by the events of life because Christ Consciousness is calm and still like the eye of a storm.

What's in It for Me?

Most of us yearn for more. Often this is experienced as wanting more things or outer events in our lives. This yearning is never truly satisfied by material things or experiences. Once you realize you *are* this Christ, you will also realize that this yearning for worldly things is simply a reflection of a deeper yearning—a yearning to be more and more your True Essence, Christ. This yearning is only satisfied by evolving your spiritual consciousness and building your awareness of the Christ you already are! A unique kind of deep satisfaction and inner peace result.

Application Examples

1. As you fulfill your yearning to be Christ through spiritually evolving and building your awareness, you will also come to know it is more a step-by-step process than an instantaneous transformation! Knowing this, you can relax and enjoy the process; like a river, it cannot be pushed!

2. In the process of applying what you have already learned and are about to learn, it may not be as smooth and easy as often believed. You can get a clue about this from the reported life of Jesus!

   a. If you notice mental, emotional or physical symptoms, you might be chemicalizing. These discomforts occur as a result of new Spiritual Truths meeting old beliefs and error thoughts. Discomforts are evidence you are doing something right; they are not evidence that you are doing something wrong.

b. You may even feel like you are being crucified! This is the crossing out of error beliefs and might even be viewed as very strong chemicalization.

c. Sooner or later you will emerge on the other side of the chemicalization and or crucifixion experience. You will feel new, resurrected, born again. In this lifetime, physical birth came first; it is followed by the second birth as you live more and more from the awareness of Oneness.

d. In moving from victim to Verity consciousness, from error to Truth, you will be regenerating your "Spiritual Self."

The Heart of the Matter

In five sentences or less, summarize the key ideas, the essence, of Chapter 4: Evolving Spiritual Awareness, Building Christ Consciousness.

_____

_____

_____

_____

_____

Putting It Into Practice

• **"Born Again"**—As you reflect on your life, within each decade pinpoint key experiences or "aha!" moments you would now identify as a growing awareness of Oneness. Notice how you changed as a result of these experiences.

_____

_____

_____

• **Chemicalization**—As you look back at the key experiences you identified in the last question, can you recall if you had any adverse physical reactions as you moved through them? Create a list of times you can remember when you had physical reactions (health challenges, emotional reactions, etc.) that correlate with the key experiences you identified.

- **Resistance and Nonresistance**—Read the following statements and notice your immediate reactions and/or mental push-back (resistance). Then practice entering into an attitude of nonresistance to the statements.

  - I Am Christ.
  - God did not create the physical universe.
  - God does not fix or change us.
  - God is not living. God is Life.
  - God is not loving. God is Love.

  - How did you master and control your thoughts and feelings of resistance in the exercise above?
  - What was crucifixion in this exercise?
  - What was resurrection in this exercise?
  - What would regeneration be?

OUR PURPOSE, DIVINE WILL, DIVINE PLAN, AND DIVINE GUIDANCE

Why Is This Important?

When we step back from our beliefs in a God that has a predetermined purpose, will, plan and guidance for us, we gain freedom. We can stop striving to determine what God's will, purpose and plan are for us. It is ironic we can believe God gives us guidance, yet this same God does not share "His" will, plan or purpose for us!

The sooner we realize there is no specific, micromanaged will, plan or purpose, the better. There is only the amorphous, nonspecific urge to be the Christ we already are. We step into our inherent power as we claim the Truth. We actually use God (Divine Ideas, Principles and Laws) to manifest our lives. The second irony is that we use what we are to be more of what we are! Charles Fillmore expressed this idea clearly during a Healing Conference in 1923, when he said: "God only does what man says he shall do. God is our servant. Did you ever think of that, that this wonderful Spirit of God, out of which everything is made is here at all times, is always present with us and we are using that God" (Lesson I, Healing Conference, 1923, pp. 28-29).

What's in It for Me?

- You will be freer of your embedded beliefs about God.
- You can let go of trying to figure God out. You can let go of wondering what God wants for you so that you can be in God's good graces.
- You will be able to focus more on living authentically from the awareness of Oneness.

Application Examples

1. In place of investing time and energy trying to please a "God out there" and discern what that external God's will, purpose and plan may be, you can now invest this time and energy in being the Christ you already are. You can know there is no specific plan. There is simply your desire to know what you are more and more, and it is yours to decide how to express It moment to moment. How this outpictures is not about God telling you how; it is about your

consciousness. Remember what Eric Butterworth said: "[God] makes no choice for you, but it is the urge and energy through which you can make the choice that is best in terms of your own consciousness … [Divine Guidance] is a wisdom, a light, a supportive flow that enables you to see the road ahead with amazing clarity and to use your own wisdom at its highest level of development" (*In the Flow of Life* by Eric Butterworth, Unity Books). It is not about waiting to know before you move forward. It is about moving forward from the awareness of "your own Knower."

2. What does your heart say you want to do? All you need to do is be centered from the Oneness and make your own choices. (See Chapter 6 in *Heart-Centered Metaphysics* for more about the Silence, and Chapter 7 for more on meditation.) Your wanting, desiring, to be a minister, doctor, teacher or plumber is not predetermined by God. However, your awareness of Oneness (Divine Mind) can help you reach your next step, based on your own consciousness. You use the Divine Urge, Energy and Wisdom (and so much more) to know the road ahead. It arises from the Divine you already are.

The Heart of the Matter

In five sentences or less, summarize the key ideas, the essence, of Chapter 5: Our Purpose, Divine Will, Divine Plan, and Divine Guidance.

_____

_____

_____

_____

_____

_____

Putting It Into Practice

• Read the following list and determine which statements reflect a God out there who determines everything and is in control, versus God/Divine Mind that is more a flow of Consciousness we use to make choices.

1. God told me to do it.
2. When I remember Oneness, I know what to say and do.
3. God blessed me.

4. I use my Divinity to bless and manifest.
5. It is in God's hands now.
6. God meant it to be this way.
7. God must have a purpose or reason for this happening in my life.
8. It's all in Divine Order.
9. If it is going to be, it is up to me.

THE SILENCE

Why Is This important?

Investing time in the Silence is how we come to feel and know that Christ is the Truth of what we are. This Christ is so much more than our ego. And, ultimately, we want to learn how to allow Christ to use our egos to be the very best we can be!

What's in It for Me?

Investing time in the Silence frees us of the whims and erratic desires of the ego and helps in the movement from victim consciousness to Verity Consciousness.

Application Examples

This chapter is more about laying the foundation of information for meditation (Chapter 7 in *Heart-Centered Metaphysics*) than it is about the application of this information. However, it can be said that each of us must apply what we come to know from investing time in the Silence. Since we each have free will, we certainly can choose not to do what is ours to do as discerned from the Silence. Further, we can confidently say investing time in the Silence results in the effect of knowing what to think, say or do. Since the Silence is a state of total nonexterior awareness, we are not aware of anything "out there" while in the Silence. The outer effect occurs after having been in the Silence.

The Heart of the Matter

In five sentences or less, summarize the key ideas, the essence, of Chapter 6: The Silence.

_____

_____

_____

_____

_____

_____

Putting It Into Practice

- Which of these occur in the Silence?

    ___ Hear voices

    ___ Light show

    ___ Nothing

    ___ Warm body sensation

    ___ No sense of time

    ___ No sensation

    ___ Visualizations

- Here is a quick and easy activity to help you discern what relaxation may feel like:

    1. Sit comfortably for a minute or two.

    2. Notice where you are feeling any tension.

    3. Tense and squeeze all the muscles in your body for a slow count of 10. Scrunch your eyes, make fists, pull in your stomach, tighten your buttocks, curl your toes. We mean *all* your muscles! Tense! Tight!

    4. Very slowly, begin to relax your muscles, allowing the tenseness to melt out through your feet.

    5. Now become aware of how you feel ... relaxed and at peace.

- Set a timer for three minutes. Sit in a comfortable position, close your eyes, and be still. Become aware of what you notice as you sit still. How are these thoughts arising in your mind? What effect do they have on sitting in the Silence?

CHAPTER SEVEN

MEDITATION

Why Is This important?

It is through the meditation that leads to the Silence that we know what we are as well as what to think, say or do. Investing time in the Silence results in a more peaceful, joyful, centered life.

What's in It for Me?

In addition to living a more peaceful, joyful and centered life, there are many other direct benefits to you. The benefits of meditation can be found on page 64 of the text *Heart-Centered Metaphysics*, as well as by searching the Internet. Some benefits of meditation include its ability to:

- Reduce anxiety—lower stress and tensions.
- Build self-confidence.
- Positively affect moods and behavior.
- Enhance energy, strength and vigor.
- Reduce heart disease.
- Facilitate weight loss.

Application Examples

1. You decide to practice Centering Prayer (a form of meditation) faithfully for at least 30 days and notice the great results you get. You create a practice consisting of at least 20 minutes once a day. Initially, you have a problem with the "monkey chatter" going on in your mind; however, you continue with your regular practice. After a week of consistent practice with Centering Prayer, you begin to notice you are more centered, less reactive, and more responsive. You realize your friends are making comments like "You seem different" or "You seem more peaceful."

2. You decide to create something to help you have a more effective experience with your Centering Prayer activities. You design a poster that vividly and colorfully displays some of the key things you want to remember, and you review it before you begin your Centering Prayer activity. The poster contains the following reminders about Centering Prayer:

   > Centering Prayer is not about actively stilling the mind or stopping my mind chatter (monkey mind). This happens as an effect of simply doing the practice. *I keep practicing!*

I am gentle with myself and begin slowly and easily. It is okay to start small and continue to add time. The important thing is to just do it!

I do not judge or evaluate my meditation time. If my ego suggests I am doing something wrong, I will say "Thank you for sharing!"

Once I have chosen my word or phrase, I stick with it. There is no such thing as the perfect word or the wrong word. The word or phrase is not as important as doing the process as described!

The Heart of the Matter

In five sentences or less, summarize the key ideas, the essence, of Chapter 7: Meditation.

_____

_____

_____

_____

_____

Putting It Into Practice

• Practice meditation for at least 30 days using the technique called "Centering Prayer" as outlined in the chapter. Keep in mind this is *not* a technique about actively shutting down or quieting the jabbering of the "monkey mind." It is about creating the practice of Centering Prayer, using a mantra you select and stick with. As a reminder, the following are some important points about the mantra you choose:

  ▪ It should be from one to seven words in length.

  ▪ It is not to be something that is commonly spoken out loud.

  ▪ It is to be used and not changed—no matter how much the ego/personality wants to change it! Jumping from mantra to mantra diminishes the effectiveness of the technique.

• Keep a journal of your experience. Notice what effect it has on your everyday life.

- Notice all the reasons you find to not meditate. Identify the things that tend to get in the way and create strategies to work around them.

CHAPTER EIGHT

PRAYER

Why Is This important?

Charles Fillmore said, "Prayer is the most accelerated form of mind action known. It steps up mental action until man's consciousness synchronizes with the Christ Mind. It is the language of spirituality. When developed, prayer makes man master in the realm of creative ideas." (*Dynamics for Living* by Charles Fillmore, Unity Books) It is through prayer we claim what is already true in the Absolute (God-Mind). Investing time in prayer is one way we take Divine Ideas from the unformed to the formed, from the invisible to the visible, from the unlimited to the limited. It is one way we step up our consciousness so that we live more and more from our Christ Nature and less from our personalities (egos).

What's in It for Me?

Similar to meditation, prayer is one way you can fulfill your potential and demonstrate more the Christ you already are. When you pray from the awareness of Oneness (Divine Mind), you are claiming the Truth of your Beingness and will become more centered and peaceful. When you are more centered and peaceful, you can more gracefully meet all that life may bring to you.

Application Examples

1. You are about to go into a meeting that has the potential to be extremely explosive and negative. You know ahead of time that other attendees disagree with your proposal. Before going into the meeting, you dedicate some quiet time using the Five-Step Prayer Method, affirming Divine Order, Wisdom, Understanding and Love. You see each person who will be attending and send them a blessing. You end with expressing gratitude for a positive meeting. You realize you are going into the meeting with a positive attitude, inner peace and clarity of mind that help you express your ideas easily and simply. The meeting goes much better than you had initially anticipated—and you can track it back to your decision to use the Five-Step Prayer Method before you went into the meeting.

2. You realize you are concerned about how you are going to pay the bills at the end of the month. Your friends' discussions about how expensive things are and how difficult it is to pay for everything have seemed to manifest in your own experience, and you realize

you are beginning to doubt the principles of Prosperity. Recognizing this, you go into a time of prayer, using the Five-Step Process. As a result, you feel more peaceful and experience a strengthened conviction about the Divine Flow of abundance. From this state, you have ideas about ways to bring in more money and are able to manifest what you need.

The Heart of the Matter

In five sentences or less, summarize the key ideas, the essence, of Chapter 8: Prayer.

_____

_____

_____

_____

_____

_____

Putting It Into Practice

• What is the difference between Affirmative Prayer and meditation?

• Read the following sentences from prayers and determine whether the statement reflects praying *to* God or reflects praying *from* the awareness of God.

  ▪ Thank you for all the blessings You have sent.

  ▪ I am grateful for the awareness of my Oneness, knowing there is no separation.

  ▪ Please send Your healing power to John as he recovers from surgery, bringing him comfort and relief.

  ▪ Dear God, help me get through this difficult time.

  ▪ The very nature of God is Love, and so I call forth that power of Love from within me, to bring harmony to my relationships.

  ▪ I affirm abundant prosperity is now flowing and I am One with Divine Ideas to manifest my good.

• Begin a daily prayer practice, using the Five-Step Prayer Process outlined in this chapter. In your journal, record your experiences, including what you find difficult as well as positive results.

• Create a table like the one shown below in which you identify the Divine Ideas you could claim, related to specific prayer requests. Then, as you invest time in the Silence, in a reflective and deliberate way, make a list of your immediate prayer requests. Before you move into the Five-Step Prayer Process, consult your table for possible Divine Ideas you may want to realize. You may also simply choose to be in the Silence and notice what eventually rises in consciousness.

Prayer request for ...	Divine Ideas to claim in relation to the request
Sickness, Illness	Wholeness, Health, Life
Lack	Abundance, Prosperity

CHAPTER NINE

PRAYING WITH OTHERS

Why Is This Important?

The bottom line of prayer is that it:

- Supports our desire for community and connection.
- Is more about the realization of the Goodness we already are than about the goodies we can get.
- Changes our consciousness and not God, Divine Mind.

What's in It for Me?

Praying with others supports you in connecting with others and being in community. This is beneficial to your well-being. What you claim in prayer for others you also claim for yourself.

Application Examples

1. You decide to practice with friends in order to get comfortable praying with others. You find that with regular practice, using a variety of realistic examples, you get more comfortable with expressing yourself out loud in prayer.

2. A friend calls you to tell you she is having surgery the next morning, and asks you to prayer with her. You use the Five-Step Prayer Process to help you share a powerful prayer with her, affirming inner peace, as well as seeing her team of physicians and surgeons operating from their highest levels of Divine Wisdom and Understanding. You give thanks for a smooth surgery and for a recovery that comes with speed, ease, comfort and joy. Your friend expresses gratitude for your inspired prayer, and you realize you were able to do it because of the structure of the Five-Step Process.

3. You want more opportunities to pray with others, so you join the prayer team at your center or church.

The Heart of the Matter

In five sentences or less, summarize the key ideas, the essence, of Chapter 9: Praying With Others.

_____

_____

_____

_____

_____

_____

Putting It Into Practice

- Select someone to be a prayer partner with you for a three-month period and schedule weekly prayer time together. (Note: After the three-month period, you may decide to continue working with your prayer partner, or you may decide to find a different one. We recommend you continue the practice of having a prayer partner with whom you can create a regular prayer practice.) Keep a journal as you move through this process, recording your fears, experiences and "aha!" moments.

- Build your awareness of the power of praying around Divine Ideas by brainstorming Divine Ideas related to the following areas:
  - Prosperity/Finance/Employment
  - Relationships
  - Healing
  - Guidance
  - Spiritual Growth

Section 2:

God—Jesus Christ— Humankind

CHAPTER TEN

BEINGNESS, ONENESS, DIVINE MIND

Why Is This Important?

The first application for all metaphysical practice is putting God first. We do not mean putting some superhuman person, being or entity first. We mean put the Truth of what you are first. Put Principle, Divine Ideas, Divine Laws, Divine Mind, Oneness, Christ Consciousness first. We always return to the awareness of Oneness, to Principle, as the starting point for any change or demonstration in our lives or the lives of others. It is the root of all Power.

Knowing the attributes or qualities of God, Principle, gives something more specific to work with and from. Simply saying "I put God first" is quite lovely and lends itself to the concept that an external, anthropomorphic God must be worshiped first. When we are more specific about what God is, we can then get a grasp on how to "use God" in the most productive ways in our everyday lives.

As you delve more and more into what God is, you will have more to work with and from. Obviously, this workbook chapter only scratches the surface. There is more about what God is in the textbook *Heart-Centered Metaphysics*, especially in Chapters 24 and 25, which focus on the Twelve Powers/Abilities.

What's in It for Me?

Once you get a glimpse of the Truth that Divine Principles, Divine Ideas, Divine Laws are entirely present and at the point of your consciousness and awareness, you will begin to step more fully into the Power and Presence you already are! These Divine Principles, Divine Ideas, Divine Laws are as present and available as natural laws, such as the law of gravity. The bottom line is you are already using them. In fact, you cannot *not* use them!

What's in it for you? You can now start using them more and more consciously. You can stop waiting on some separate God to do for you what you must do for yourself!

Application Examples

1. The Truth of you is this Beingness, Christ Nature, you live *from*. God is not a Being you wait upon. In this context, you are not waiting upon a separate God to solve your life situations or to bless you in some way. You are waiting upon the awareness of Divine Idea(s)

you will use to meet the situation for the highest good of all or to bring a blessing into your life. In a way, you begin to "use God" instead of God using you or doing something to you or for you. When you find yourself in a bit of a fix, you do not have to wait for God to do something for you or to you. You use your own Divine Nature to see it differently. You can ask yourself, "How do I use even this to become more aware there is only One Power and One Presence? How do I use this to demonstrate I am Christ?"

2. When you know you are Divine, you are Absolute Good, the All Good, then you will know you can apply Divine Ideas, Laws and Principles to your life to manifest good. You *are* the Power and Presence that can take anything, *anything*, in the relative realm and use it for good and to bring forth blessings. If you get a diagnosis of some illness, experience a divorce, or undergo any other difficult situation, you can be assured you have It in you to use it all for good!

3. It is easy to apply the concepts that "God is our Source, Supply, Substance" when you know what they mean. You may think God is literally the source and supply of everything in the Absolute Realm and the relative realm. You may think God is the physical substance as well as Spiritual Substance. However, you will step more fully into your Power when you realize "God is our Source, Supply and Substance" of Divine Ideas, and *only* Divine ideas. It is your responsibility to use these Divine Ideas to manifest your good! You have absolute dominion of these Divine Ideas. You use Divine Laws like the Law of Divine Order (Mind-Idea-Expression/mind-idea-expression) to manifest your life. If you get a diagnosis of some illness, you get centered and remain still until the awareness of an Idea/idea arises in consciousness. It is then yours to bring that Idea/idea from the level of consciousness into the world of form. You are the transformer of the infinite to the finite, the formless to the formed.

4. God is Principle and Law. When you experience a loss—for example, a divorce or loved one's transition—you can know Divine Principle and Law are available. You can know Divine Ideas are fully present, ready to be used. You can manifest from them using the Law of Cause and Effect/Law of Divine Order, which is Mind-Idea-Expression. You can know God is Love and God is Strength. There is no waiting for a God out there to bestow them upon you or give them to you according to His whim. These Divine Ideas are fully present at the point of your consciousness and awareness. Use them! The Divine Idea of Love is used to feel comfort and bring har-

mony. The Divine Idea of Strength is used to be strong and to have the fortitude to move through loss.

The Heart of the Matter

In five sentences or less, summarize the key ideas, the essence, of Chapter 10: Beingness, Oneness, Divine Mind.

_____

_____

_____

_____

_____

_____

Putting It Into Practice

• Think back to the God of your childhood. Journal a description of what that God was like, as best you can recall.

• How is the God of your childhood different from your understanding of God after reading this chapter? Journal about that.

• Based on your new understanding of God, rewrite the Lord's Prayer.

CHAPTER ELEVEN

THE SPIRITUAL UNIVERSE AND THE PHYSICAL UNIVERSE

Why Is This Important?

Once we understand God is not directly manifesting the physical universe, we can begin to understand what we can do instead of waiting for God to do something for us.

God not directly manifesting the physical universe is fundamental to affirmative prayer, the Unity way of prayer. Think about it. If we believe God made and is manifesting the physical universe, then it would be appropriate to ask and beseech God to change and manipulate it in our favor. In Unity, we pray from the awareness of God, or Principle. We do not pray *to* God. We claim what is already True in the Absolute Realm or God. And then we act on it!

What's in It for Me?

Once you know the God of your childhood does not exist as you had thought, you know the Truth and can claim the Power to make it manifest from the Absolute to the relative realm in consciousness, and finally out into the physical realm if you so choose. You no longer wait for the God of your childhood to fix things, give things, or punish you in some capricious, unpredictable way.

Application Examples

1. Now when you are sick, you no longer ask God to heal you; you claim the Absolute Truth of Wholeness and Life. You visualize this Life radiating from the infinite and expressing at the finite point of your physical body. When you know you are the one manifesting your body according to your consciousness and collective consciousness, you know changing your consciousness can and does change the outer manifestation.

2. If you are manifesting lack, you can now know that God, Divine Principle, cannot and does not visit lack on people or take things away in some fit of displeasure. If you are manifesting lack, there is something in consciousness (individual or collective consciousness) limiting the Infinite and resulting in lack. When you have lack thoughts, an "abundance of lack shows up!" It is your respon-

sibility to get still and know the Truth—God is Abundance. God is the very principle of Prosperity!

How do we know this? Consider a simple idea in the relative realm—the idea of a table. Even in this relative realm, the idea of a table demonstrates the principles of Abundance and Prosperity. The idea of a table can never be used up. The idea of a table can be expressed in an infinite number of ways. That's prosperity; that's abundance! Now think about this: God is Divine Mind made up entirely of Divine Ideas and the concomitant Laws and Principles to bring them forth. Divine Ideas can never be used up, and Divine Ideas can be used in an infinite number of ways according to the consciousness using them. Abundance! Prosperity!

If you are experiencing lack, you realize it is your responsibility to become aware of the Divine Idea(s) fulfilling the need. Once aware of It, *you* bring It into expression. You bring It from the Absolute to the relative realm clothing It in form.

3. Whatever the situation, challenge or even opportunity, you recognize it is your responsibility to discern the degree to which you are depending on sense consciousness to manifest the results you want. The more you rely on sense consciousness, the less you will be aware of your Divine Nature; the less you will be aware of Divine Ideas. You ask yourself: Am I going to believe my senses? Or am I going to place my trust, my faith in the Goodness I already am?

The Heart of the Matter

In five sentences or less, summarize the key ideas, the essence, of Chapter 11: The Spiritual Universe and the Physical Universe.

_____

_____

_____

_____

_____

_____

Putting It Into Practice

- Go outside at night and take a long look at the stars. Reflect on the following question: What does it mean at a deep level to understand that an anthropomorphic God did not create the universe?

- Open a new can of Play Doh. (Go ahead and smell it! We'll wait!) Spend some time creating something with your Play Doh. Once you are through, reflect on how you created this object from an idea in your mind. How is this similar to the way the universe was created?

CHAPTER TWELVE

THE DIVINE PARADOXES

Why Is This Important?

The concepts "God is Principle; God is personal" are important because this realization gets us away from the personification of God. "God is personal" gives us the awareness that each of us creates/manifests an experience of God based on and from our own consciousness.

The concepts "God is transcendent; God is immanent" are important because while we know "God is out there," we can also know God (Principle or Divine Mind) is right here, immanent. We do not have to call upon a faraway God. In a sense, God is not a long-distance call; God is a local call ... a local awareness.

The concepts "God as mother; God as father" help us to move a step away from the concept that God is a being with parts, like a man or a woman! God is not a male deity or a female deity (a goddess). We recognize the Divine, our True Nature, having qualities we associate with being mother or father. God as mother means God, Divine Mind, has qualities like a mother. God as father means God, Divine Mind, has qualities like a father. God is *neither* mother *nor* father. Further, this somewhat artificial grouping of qualities under the labels "mother" and "father" is culturally determined and thus varies from culture to culture. You have Divine Qualities that are motherlike and fatherlike as determined by your own concepts of mother and father.

The concepts "God is Law; God is grace" are important. We are not referring to grace in the traditional way: the free and unmerited favor of God, as manifested in the salvation of sinners and the bestowal of blessings. God, Principle, is not simply a hard and fast law. Goodness, Principle, is always available and can always trump Law. On one hand it is our ability to change our minds; on the other, just as collective consciousness can have an untoward effect on us, it can also have a positive and supportive effect. You can reap in fields where you did not sow.

What's in It for Me?

Divine Ideas are right where you already are! The concepts "God is transcendent; God is immanent" allow you to know you do not have to beseech or reach out to some external God. You know It is totally present at the point of your awareness. Thinking you have to ask an external God for something is much like thinking you have to go to the Wal-Mart across town to get toothpaste, when all the while you are standing looking at the toothpaste in your local Wal-Mart!

You are *not* confined or defined by your physical gender! "God as mother; God as father" helps you know you have all you need right where you are. Do you want to be fatherlike? The Divine Ideas or Qualities you define or perceive as "fatherly" are already present at the point of your awareness! Do you want to be motherlike? The Divine Ideas or Qualities you define or perceive as "motherly" are already present at the point of your awareness!

You are always using the Law. Grace is always available because you can change your mind in a heartbeat. Further, sometimes you do not reap all you sow because you reap good from fields where you have not sown! There are benefits garnered from the more positive aspects of collective consciousness.

Application Examples

1. Whatever the situation, event or good you want to express, Principle is always available because It is the Truth of what you are. It is your Consciousness. You use It. In the process, you can choose to have whatever experience of God, Divine Mind, you desire. You create your personal experience of It. Ironically, you must be using Principle from the level of consciousness you are able to "muster" at the present moment. It is there no matter how you choose to react or respond to a divorce, diagnosis or other situation in your life. As you go through the experience, *you* create your experience of your Divine Nature. It can be anything from a loving, supportive Presence to even feeling like It has abandoned you!

2. You have the full range of Divine Ideas, Principles and Laws to apply to your life according to your consciousness. You do not have to beg or ask God to give them to you. They already *are* you, the Truth of what you are! Name the problem, situation or event. You can be sure there are Divine Ideas, Principles and Laws you can apply to be the Christ you already are and manifest good and blessings for others as well as yourself.

3. Many situations and events may require you to be "motherlike" at one moment and then "fatherlike" in the next. Your response to these situations and events is not limited by your physical gender. It is only limited by your awareness of the Divine Qualities and Divine Ideas categorized as motherlike or fatherlike according to your personal perceptions as well as cultural biases.

4. Again, no matter the situation or event in your life, the Law is available at the point of your consciousness; grace, the higher

octave of the Law, is absolutely and simultaneously totally available. If you make a choice and you do not like it or how it feels—make another choice!

The Heart of the Matter

In five sentences or less, summarize the key ideas, the essence, of Chapter 12: The Divine Paradoxes.

_____

_____

_____

_____

_____

Putting It Into Practice

- How do you experience God in a personal way? Capture your ideas in your journal. How does this align with what you know about God from studying Chapter 10: Beingness, Oneness, Divine Mind?

- Choose one of the Four Paradoxes identified in Chapter 12 and invest one week looking for specific examples of how it shows up in your life. Capture your thoughts in your journal about the impact this paradox has on you in terms of your daily living.

CHAPTER THIRTEEN

THE TRINITY

Why Is this Important?

The metaphysical trinity (Mind-Idea-Expression) is based on the traditional Holy Trinity (Father-Son-Holy Spirit). Mind-Idea-Expression is how everything—yes, we said *everything*—comes into existence. It is a more clearly defined example of the Law of Cause and Effect. It is how infinite and unlimited Divine Ideas are brought into the relative realm, moving from infinite to finite, unformed to formed according to our consciousness.

What's in It for Me?

You will have a better experience of life if you learn to use this law consciously, from a higher awareness of the Divine you already are. Once again, it is not a matter of choosing to use it or not. You cannot *not* use Divine Order! You are always using this creative law, this creative sequence: first, Mind-Idea-Expression, then, mind-idea-expression.

Clearly, you may use Divine Order consciously or unconsciously, from sense consciousness or from higher consciousness. Do you want something in your life? Use the metaphysical interpretation of the Trinity (mind-idea-expression) to make it happen.

Application Examples

1. Let's say you want to create a nonprofit organization to help older children be adopted. You have the big idea; now it is yours to bring into expression. The idea is first in consciousness. You give it more form in consciousness by adding other ideas and thoughts. Finally, you manifest it in the physical realm based on the thought forms you are holding in consciousness. You will use many—most likely all—of your Twelve Powers (Chapters 24 and 25) to "manifest" the idea in your consciousness—to give it form. You will undoubtedly become aware of other Divine Ideas from which you derive relative ideas and thoughts for manifesting the idea—all the while using the Law of Divine Order based on the metaphysical trinity (Mind-Idea-Expression/mind-idea-expression). You are using the orderly process by which everything comes into existence.

2. Sometimes you use the Law of Divine Order to simply enjoy or relive a memory. Something, like the smell of a pumpkin pie or a turkey baking in the oven, might remind you of a trip to grandma's house. You are recalling a cherished memory in the present about

the past. You simply have a vivid experience of that time from the past in this now moment. It is happening entirely in your own consciousness.

3.   Later, you might recall the memory again. However, this time you decide to bake the pumpkin pie from your grandmother's recipe.

The Heart of the Matter

In five sentences or less, summarize the key ideas, the essence, of Chapter 13: The Trinity.

_____

_____

_____

_____

_____

Putting It Into Practice

• Make yourself a peanut butter and jelly sandwich. Using the sandwich as a metaphor, relate it to the concept of the Trinity as discussed in Chapter 13.

• As you go through your normal day, be on the lookout for experiences of Mind-Idea-Expression at work.

CHAPTER FOURTEEN

SIN, EVIL AND THE DEVIL

Why Is This Important?

Some of us were raised with the concept of "unforgivable sin," or at least, our sins are only purged by the sacrifice Jesus made for us ("washed in the blood of Jesus!"). While we may "sin" (make errors), these errors are correctable.

Further, there is the widespread belief that evil is Real and is instigated by the Devil. However, when we know evil is nothing more than sin (error) being repeated over and over again, we can simply wake up and stop the errors. The "Devil," or "Satan," is not an entity or being. It is nothing more than the build-up of sin/error in collective consciousness. It only seems to have a pull on us and only to the degree we empower it!

Finally, once we know Hell is a state of consciousness, we can release ourselves from a fear of Hell. It is not a place we are banished to as God's punishment for our sins. Hell is simply the discomfort we feel as a result of sin/evil/error. Likewise, Heaven is not a place we go to as a reward for living a "godly life." It is a state of consciousness when we are centered and feel peace and joy as a result of living from a higher state of spiritual awareness.

What's in It for Me?

Dare we say everything? What's in it for you is the experience of being the best person or Christ you can be! Self-awareness and self-knowledge (Chapter 2) of the errors of your ways can lead to changing your mind and stepping away from sin (error), resulting in a more heavenly awareness. The less you sin (make errors), the less evil there is. Also, the collective consciousness has less error, thus lessening any power we have been giving it.

You no longer fear the "Devil" or "Satan" because you realize there is no external entity influencing or having power over you. You realize you are, in fact, diminishing the built up error in collective consciousness.

Application Examples

1. The cartoons showing a devil on one shoulder and an angel on the other were not far from the truth (little "t"). You have probably experienced being pulled in two different directions when faced with a moral decision, or what might be called a decision of consciousness. There seems to be a "devil" urging you to be bad ... to error ... to sin. While, at the same time, there seems to be another

voice, "an angel" encouraging you to be the best you can be! Which wins? Who chooses? You! You might ask, Who is the "you" that chooses? This would be your independent observer.

If you decide with "the devil," or error consciousness, you will strengthen it. You will give it more power. You will "sin." You will make a choice that lowers your consciousness. This choice also tends to lower the collective consciousness.

If you decide with "the angel, or higher consciousness," you will "strengthen it." You will give it more power. You make a choice raising your consciousness and the collective consciousness at the same time.

For example, let's say you are having difficulty taking a test. You notice you can see another student's answers from where you are seated. Your "devil" encourages you to look at those answers. It seems to say, "Go ahead, no one is watching ... who's gonna know?" At the same time, your "angel" is encouraging you to do the best you can on the test, to stay in integrity, and not to cheat. Which one do you choose? Which one do you strengthen?

2. As a child, you may have been tempted to shoplift a piece of candy. The little devil on your shoulder may have said, "Come on, you can do it, you know you want that candy ... nobody will know." Your angel, the voice of morality, integrity and a higher consciousness may have said, "Pay for the candy; do the right thing!" If you take it and do not get caught, you will tempt yourself to do it again and again ... until you wake up—or get caught!

The Heart of the Matter

In five sentences or less, summarize the key ideas, the essence, of Chapter 14: Sin, Evil and the Devil.

_____

_____

_____

_____

_____

Putting It Into Practice

• Go for a bicycle ride. Enjoy the excursion! While you are riding, become aware of how often you are self-correcting to stay on your desired course. When you get back home, take some time to journal about how this awareness of constantly self-correcting as you ride a bicycle is similar to how you self-correct when you "sin" (miss the mark) or are tempted to "sin."

• Draw a picture of how you feel when you are having a "hell" experience. Now transform that picture into the way you feel when you are able to change your consciousness and turn it into a "heaven" experience. Reflect on the feelings you experienced as you did this activity—and what it tells you about your life situations.

JESUS, THE CHRIST, JESUS CHRIST, CHRIST JESUS

Why Is This Important?

Jesus—Jesus was not unique in the sense of being the only Son of God. Jesus was a man, flesh and blood just like you and me. Jesus had human consciousness. He had temptations just like we do. The difference is this: He became aware of his True Divine Nature, Christ, and went about developing it, expressing it, and living from this awareness.

The Christ—The Christ is not a synonym for Jesus. It is a synonym for God or God Nature. It is your True Consciousness.

Jesus Christ—This combination recognizes the integration that occurred when Jesus, the man, was fully living from Christ Consciousness. And yet, human consciousness was still present (as exemplified by his angst in the Garden of Gethsemane prior to his crucifixion). This is important because all of us can realize this level of Christ Consciousness here and now.

Christ Jesus—At and following the Ascension of our Consciousness to Its highest, most elevated level, there is simply Christ Consciousness. No human consciousness remains.

What's in It for Me?

Simple: You are not defined or limited by your simple humanity (personality/ego and body). If Jesus did it, you can do it. What he did you could be doing or even more, if his words as reported in the Christian Scriptures are true.

You can also know that learning to live from Christ Consciousness is a process, so be easy on yourself. Realizing Christ Consciousness is not usually attained in an instant; it is not an instantaneous thing.

Application Examples

1. You are in a bit of a hurry and decide to pick up a few last-minute items at the grocery store. You pick the shortest line. The customer in front of you has an item that is not priced causing the need to call for a manager. You begin to think this always happens to you. After the order is complete, the customer pulls out a handful of coupons. You begin to roll your eyes, wondering how long this is going to take. Just then, you remember you are not a "who" (a personality with a body): you are, metaphorically, "Jesus." You

remember "what" you are: Christ. You take a deep breath and begin to relax into the now moment. Instead of flashing the customer a look that could kill, you simply smile and bid her a good day.

2. You are driving to an appointment to see your lawyer and run smack into a traffic jam. Just when you are starting to make progress, a car rudely cuts in front of you. You are at a choice point. You can choose to pound on your horn and wave your fist, or you can choose to remain quiet, sending the driver a blessing to affirm peace and the highest and best. Which do you choose—and what is being reflected?

In any decision, it is always best to pause and reflect on whether your decisions are being made drawing upon Christ Consciousness or from human consciousness (sense consciousness). When you call upon Christ Consciousness in a sustained way, you strengthen your awareness of It. This helps you more fully be the Christ you already are.

As you will recall from the last chapter, your "devil" desires to be unkind while your "angel" wants to simply be kind and loving. You decide to take a deep breath and pause. You decide to remember, yes, you have an ego and a body (sense consciousness, or metaphorically, "Jesus"). You also remember there is "that" of you, Christ, always coming from the highest and best. You decide to demonstrate to yourself and the other driver you know you are Christ by responding with kindness and love.

You've taken action to prove, whatever your human name, you are _____ Christ. (Fill in the blank with your name.) As you do this more and more, you respond more and more automatically from your Christ nature and less and less from your ego/personality (sense consciousness, or metaphorically, "Jesus"). You are metaphysically and metaphorically becoming "Christ Jesus," or Christ _____. (Again, you fill in the blank.)

The Heart of the Matter

In five sentences or less, summarize the key ideas, the essence, of Chapter 15: Jesus, the Christ, Jesus Christ, Christ Jesus.

_____

_____

_____

_____

_____

_____

Putting It Into Practice

• Create two separate and distinct introductions for yourself as if you were being introduced to an audience. Write the first one presenting your ego/personality. Write the second one introducing you as the Christ you already are!

• For one full day, respond to every situation by being the best Christ you can be! Capture your experiences and feelings about this activity in your journal.

CHAPTER SIXTEEN

THE THREEFOLD NATURE OF HUMANKIND—SPIRIT, SOUL AND BODY

Why Is This Important?

Our threefold nature is important for many of the same reasons as already stated in earlier chapters. We are Spirit, soul and body.

- We are Spirit is another way of saying we are God, Christ, as well as Superconscious Mind. Knowing this, we are aware we do not have to earn It or beg for It. We are already It—Spirit. It is a matter of waking up to It, realizing It, and living from the awareness or consciousness of It.

- Knowing we are soul is the same as saying we are Jesus in the sense we seem to have a mind made of conscious and subconscious minds. The soul or mind is highly influenced by the information gained from our senses, or sense consciousness, if we so choose. And, let's be clear, we do decide whether the choice is conscious or not.

  The body is both the "precipitation of the thinking part of man [individual and collective]" as well as the vehicle from which the five senses operate (*The Revealing Word* by Charles Fillmore, Unity Books). It is the effect of consciousness as well as a puppet of consciousness.

What's in It for Me?

This is another way to recognize your humanity, your ego/personality and your body while knowing "what" you are is the Absolute Truth, Spirit. It is not about denying your ego/personality or body; it is about working with your ego/personality so you can be the best person or Christ you can be.

Application Example

You notice you've been gaining weight. Since you know that the body is an effect of consciousness, you know you must change something in consciousness instead of simply doing something in the outer realm. You become still and realize you have been under a lot of stress and eating fairly unconsciously. You do some stress release self-care by meditating more

(Spirit) and become more conscious (soul/mind) about all the food you eat (body). You also begin keeping a food diary, recording what you eat. You easily lose the 10 pounds you had gained.

The Heart of the Matter

In five sentences or less, summarize the key ideas, the essence, of Chapter 16: The Threefold Nature of Humankind.

_____

_____

_____

_____

_____

_____

Putting It Into Practice

• During your daily morning meditation, purposely reflect on the following three questions:

- What am I going to do today to take care of my body?
- What am I going to do today to take care of my soul (mind)?
- What am I going to do today to remember I am Spirit?

• Take action on the Divine Ideas that come. Capture the impact of your choices in your journal.

CHAPTER SEVENTEEN

THE THREE PHASES OF MIND

Why Is This Important?

Once we become aware of the fact that our conscious and subconscious minds are of the relative realm, we can depend on them changing. The good news is we can use this changeability to our advantage. We can change any of our limiting or erroneous relative thoughts, habits and feelings.

Life goes better when we invest time in the Silence and allow the Superconscious Mind to infuse the subconscious mind with Divine Ideas, thus impacting the conscious mind. We can also limit the degree to which we impress the subconscious mind from the conscious mind and our senses.

What's in It for Me?

When you know how the three phases of mind work together, you can consciously begin a process of literally upgrading your subconscious mind. Since the subconscious mind impacts the conscious mind, you will consciously live more productively.

Application Examples

1. Let's say over time, you become aware of living in a state of lack. You find it difficult to make ends meet; there's too much month left after the money runs out! With focused self-awareness and observation, you are able to surface some long-standing beliefs you had been holding in your subconscious mind. Once aware of this belief, you can begin using your conscious mind to reprogram your subconscious mind. At the same time you disempower the limiting belief(s), you also empower prosperous beliefs. Through investing time in the Silence, the Superconscious Mind works to also clear the limiting belief(s).

2. Perhaps you become aware of a belief you chose as a child: a belief that you do not value yourself because of comments and criticism coming from your parents, teachers and maybe even friends. You notice how you always put others first to your own detriment. Upon self-reflection and introspection, you become aware of this belief that you have no value. Once you can articulate the belief as precisely as possible, you will be able to use your conscious mind and Superconscious Mind to reprogram your subconscious mind.

The Heart of the Matter

In five sentences or less, summarize the key ideas, the essence, of Chapter 17: The Three Phases of Mind.

_____

_____

_____

_____

_____

_____

Putting It Into Practice

• Create your own personal guided meditation that takes you on a journey through three levels. (Examples might be a cave experience, diving into a pond or river, or climbing a mountain.) Once you have written this meditation, present it to a small group and ask for their feedback in terms of how they experienced it.

CHAPTER EIGHTEEN

PERSONALITY/INDIVIDUALITY

Why Is This Important?

This is important because the personality is something we make up while our Individuality is what we already are, in Truth.

What's in It for Me?

When you are aware your personality does not choose you, it is not genetic, and you are actually making it up, you can begin modifying or eliminating those parts of your personality that do not serve you well. Those unproductive parts of your ego are collectively termed your adverse ego. It is adverse to your being the best person or Christ you can be.

Know that your Individuality is assured because you already are, in Truth, Christ (the Idea that is made up of Ideas). You can develop those aspects of Individuality of which you are already aware as well as discover other aspects of your Individuality of which you were unaware. Aspects of our Individuality include the Twelve Powers/Abilities. You may want to review these in more detail by referring to Chapters 25 and 26 in *Heart-Centered Metaphysics*.

Application Examples

1. You are in a meeting and begin to notice how you are responding to someone else. As you do so, you notice some harsh judgments you have about him. As the meeting proceeds, you also notice a "tone" in your voice whenever you must respond to him. In fact, you find yourself reacting rather than responding. As you observe this behavior, you begin to realize that adverse aspects of your personality are showing up. For some reason you are choosing to react from this clearly unproductive part of your personality. Once aware of this, you begin to take action to transform or eliminate whatever it is you were reacting from. You choose to be different and to live more and more from the awareness of your Individuality.

2. As you reflect on a situation from your own life similar to number 1 above, notice it is another aspect of your personality actually doing the choosing to observe and be different. This could be called your supportive ego. Notice also how you use the supportive aspects of your ego/personality to be a better person or the Christ you already are. Charles Fillmore said, "The ego of itself is possessed of nothing. It is a mere ignorant child of innocence floating

in the Mind of Being, but through the door of its consciousness must pass all the treasures of God" (*Keep a True Lent,* p. 55).

The Heart of the Matter

In five sentences or less, summarize the key ideas, the essence, of Chapter 18: Personality/Individuality.

_____

_____

_____

_____

_____

_____

Putting It Into Practice

• Gather lots of creative tools, such as markers, paint, ribbon, yarn, paste, paper plates, brown paper bags. Using these tools, create a mask that reflects something about your personality.

• Put your mask on or over some kind of light, and reflect on how the mask affects the light. Now respond to the following question:

Imagine the light reflects your Higher Self, while the mask you created represents your personality/ego, which is the "bushel basket" you hold over your light that keeps it from shining as brightly as it can. What does your bushel basket look like—and what can you do to let your light shine?

Section 3:

The Basic Tool Kit for Living

CHAPTER NINETEEN

THE FOUR FUNCTIONS OF CONSCIOUSNESS

Why Is This Important?

The four functions of consciousness are the ways in which we deal with and manage our interactions with the outer realm. We think, feel, sense and intuit.

What's in It for Me?

When you know you have these four methods of interfacing with the world, you not only have more control, but also more ways to deal with the outer realm. Until you are aware of these four functions of consciousness, you are probably interacting with the world primarily from one or maybe two of them. Surely, four ways are better than one or two.

Application Examples

1. Let's say your preferred way of interacting with the world is by way of your feeling function. You find yourself in what seems to be a totally new situation. Yet below conscious awareness, it reminds you of other situations that did not turn out well. As you proceed, you feel fearful (feeling function). If you are unaware you have the three other functions of consciousness, you will simply succumb to your fear. However, if you are aware of your thinking, sensing and intuiting natures, you can bring them into play. Your sensing function provides information via your five senses, while your thinking nature rationally analyzes the information received from your senses. Using your intuiting function, you can meet this new situation from a higher level of consciousness. A higher wisdom is engaged.

The Heart of the Matter

In five sentences or less, summarize the key ideas, the essence, of Chapter 19: The Four Functions of Consciousness.

_____

_____

_____

_____

_____

_____

Putting It Into Practice

• Over the course of several days, simply observe how you interact with the world around you. Discern which of the four functions you use the most. You might even rank them from the most to the least used. Once you are aware of the function(s) you primarily use, you can then begin to consciously practice using the others. Your goal is to use all four in the most balanced way possible.

• The next time you notice your feeling nature is strongly engaged, try this:

    A. *Feeling*: Simply allow yourself to be aware of the feelings, noticing how you are experiencing these feelings.

    B. *Sensing*: Be aware of what information you are gleaning from your senses. What are you hearing, seeing, smelling, touching, tasting?

    C. *Thinking*: Rationally look at the information you are getting from your senses, and reflect on times you had a similar reaction. What are you believing now that is the impetus for what you are feeling?

    D. *Intuiting*: Get still, breathe and center yourself. If you have time, meditate for awhile and notice if any new ideas or thoughts pop into your awareness. How are you going to use these ideas to change your experience?

• As a way to heighten your awareness of the four functions of consciousness, practice the art of "The Four Questions." Throughout your day, periodically stop in the midst of whatever situation you're involved in, pause, and ask yourself these four questions:

1. What am I thinking?
2. What I am feeling?
3. What am I sensing?
4. What am I intuiting?

• The order in which you ask them is not important; just be sure you explore all four questions. Next, reflect on what you are experiencing in a deliberate, balanced way. You might notice you need to more consciously increase your use of one function or another.

CHAPTER TWENTY

THOUGHT/FEELING

Why Is This Important?

First, all these teachings and their applications work together. This is especially true of Chapter 20, "Thought/Feeling" and the next three chapters: "The Word"; "Denials and Affirmations"; and "Creation."

Once we understand that a thought does not always precede every feeling, we can better understand how we interact with the outer world, as well as how we experience the "inner realm" of consciousness. When we believed a thought led to every feeling, it seemed we had absolute control over our feeling nature. The discovery that feelings can and often do precede thoughts certainly changes our view. Even so, we can still use feelings to discover what we are thinking—and vice versa. Thoughts cause feelings. Feelings cause thoughts. Perhaps thoughts and feelings occur together.

We manifest by the Law of Mind Action: Thoughts held in mind produce after their kind. It is important to grasp the true meaning of this Law. It is not merely thought; it is more like thoughts with feelings produce after their kind. It is important to realize both thinking and feeling need to be engaged in order to manifest or demonstrate. Through thought and feeling, we have dominion over Divine Ideas and, most especially, our own consciousness.

What's in It for Me?

You are not a victim of your own mind, thoughts and/or feelings. You are not even at their mercy, nor are you at the mercy of Divine Ideas. You have total dominion. You choose, moment to moment, what you master or to what degree you abdicate your power.

Application Examples

1. You have recurring thoughts about an extremely unsatisfactory interaction with a co-worker. At first, it seems like you have no power or control over this thinking pattern. It seems to control you. Eventually, you recall the Law of Mind Action; at this point, you choose to assume control over this repetitious thinking/feeling pattern. After all, these thoughts keep repeating *because* of the Law of Mind Action. Each time you repeat these thoughts and feelings, you have the same thoughts and feelings again and again—until you do something to intervene and change the thought pattern. You gain control when you choose new thoughts and engage your feeling nature more productively.

2. You notice you have a certain uncomfortable feeling whenever you find yourself in a certain type of situation (for example, working with a specific individual or dealing with a certain type of task). As soon as you are aware of the feeling, you consciously apply your thinking and feeling nature to stop the unwanted feelings. Or you may choose to pause and "dive into" the feeling with the intention of discovering if there is anything behind it. You want to discover if there is an underlying cause. Once the cause is identified, you can go to work on it using the various metaphysical laws you are studying. (You can read more about the Power of the Word, and Denials and Affirmations in Chapters 21 and 22 of *Heart-Centered Metaphysics*.)

The Heart of the Matter

In five sentences or less, summarize the key ideas, the essence, of Chapter 20: Thought/Feeling.

_____

_____

_____

_____

_____

Putting It Into Practice

• Become aware of a situation where you notice you are having undesirable, uncomfortable thoughts (for example, you planned a golf game and it is raining. You are thinking, "What a bummer! Why does it have to rain the one day I want to play golf?"). As soon as you become aware of your thoughts, identify what feelings are going along with those thoughts. Consciously change the thought. How does that affect your feelings?

• Become aware of a situation in which you realize you are feeling uncomfortable. (For example, you are in a meeting and your idea was shot down by others. You realize your fists are clenched, your stomach is queasy, and you are feeling a warm flush to your face). As soon as you become aware of your feelings, identify what thoughts are accompanying them. Consciously change the feeling (by taking a couple of slow, deep breaths, for example, or relaxing your hands, rolling your shoulders) and notice how the change affects your thoughts.

CHAPTER TWENTY-ONE

THE WORD

Why Is This Important?

This chapter works with the previous chapter ("Thought/Feeling") and the two that follow ("Denials and Affirmations" and "Creation").

Whether spoken to oneself or out loud, it is the Power of the Word that fuels our thoughts and feelings. This chapter gives us a more concrete reason and method for having dominion over our thoughts and feelings. The Word and the Power of the Word are "how-tos" for gaining control and mastery over consciousness. The Power of the Word derives from the Divine Ideas making up our innate Christ Nature. When we use Divine Ideas, they are colored and modified by collective consciousness as well as individual consciousness.

What's in It for Me?

Plenty! However, first be aware that you delude yourself if you believe you are becoming aware of pure, unadulterated Divine Ideas. You will be more deliberate and, yes, maybe even more cautious when you understand that collective consciousness and individual consciousness are involved in the process. Being aware of this helps you more easily discern the degree to which you are engaging the ego and sense consciousness rather than higher levels of consciousness. This awareness leads to the heightened possibility of using Divine Ideas in potentially purer ways. Ultimately, you will be able to be a better person and more the Christ you already are.

Application Examples

1. You are seeking a solution to a problem and decide to invest some time in the Silence to discern ideas you can use to deal with it. It's not that you are actually becoming aware of the pure Divine Ideas themselves, but more like you are becoming aware of ideas and thoughts related to Divine Ideas. You are seeking an inspired idea, thought or guidance from your Higher Self. Since you know every Divine Idea is altered and colored by collective and individual consciousness, you can be on the alert to what your ego/personality might add to the thought or idea. You can then use the Power of the Word consciously and perhaps more purely to stick with the highest thought or idea.

2. You get the call to be a minister. You hear your inner voice saying something like "apply to ministerial school." Almost immediately, your ego/personality starts adding to the call. You assume you will be a minister; you fantasize and imagine yourself being a minister; you begin wondering what churches would be ideal for you to serve as minister. At some point, you notice you have added to the original thought or idea. The thought was simply "apply to ministerial school." It was not "I am going to be a minister." At this point, you can use the Power of the Word to refocus on the original information rather than adding to it. From here, you can use the Power of the Word to keep yourself on track and simply do what you need to do to apply to ministerial school.

The Heart of the Matter

In five sentences or less, summarize the key ideas, the essence, of Chapter 21: The Word.

_____

_____

_____

_____

_____

_____

Putting It Into Practice

• Employ the *Backward Glance Technique,* using the following chart to help you.

The Christ/Divine Ideas	Thoughts/Feelings	Words you associate with this activity/event

Directions:

  a. Think about an activity you are excited about. Begin at the **far right side** of the chart and identify words you associate with this activity.

  b. As you focus on those words, what thoughts and feelings are triggered? Fill these in under the "Thoughts/Feelings" column.

  d. As you reflect on these thoughts and feelings, what Divine Idea is at the foundation of the activity you are working on? As you work backward, you can begin to recognize that every activity can be traced back to The Christ/Divine Ideas.

- Using the same Backward Glance chart, think about a situation you perceive as negative (for instance, an upsetting conversation with a friend). Become aware as you capture the words associated with the activity, along with the thoughts and feelings, what Divine Idea this situation is based on. Then consider how you could change your thoughts/feelings and words to impact the outcome in a more positive way.

- When you find yourself in a conversation about the economy, and realize it is spiraling negatively, find a way to shift the consciousness of the conversation. Become aware of your own thoughts and feelings as you focus on different words to interject into the conversation.

CHAPTER TWENTY-TWO

DENIALS AND AFFIRMATIONS

Why Is This Important?

In short, denials and affirmations are "consciousness conditioners." Denials are for disempowering unwanted thoughts, beliefs and feelings. Affirmations are for claiming Divine Ideas, Divine Truths, in consciousness. When you claim realized Truth, it is more and more likely that you will be those Ideas and Truths, live them, and express them.

What's in It for Me?

Denials and affirmations are the tools you use in the application of the Law of Mind Action and the Power of the Word. With these powerful tools, you can change your mind, your thoughts and your feelings. You use your innate dominion to be and do what you want—hopefully, to be a better person and, ultimately, the Christ you already are.

Application Examples

1. Think back to your experience in Chapter 20, when you had recurring thoughts and feelings about an unsatisfactory interaction with a co-worker. In this application example, you call on denials and affirmations to change your thoughts and feelings. You employ denials to disempower the repetitious thoughts and feelings you are having. As soon as you are aware of the repetitious thought, you say to yourself, "I dissolve all power I give to these thoughts and feelings." You then apply a realized Truth via an affirmation to shift your focus and establish a new thinking pattern in place of the one you do not want. For example, "In this present moment, I am poised and joyful."

2. You apply denials and affirmations in any situation where you notice you are having a feeling you do not want. You deny giving power to the feeling as soon as you are aware of it. For example, let's say the feelings are stress and anxiety. You might say, "I give no power to any feelings of stress and anxiety." Next, you claim a realized Truth to affirm an appropriate thought and feeling. In the case of feeling stress and anxiety, you might realize and affirm, "I am Christ, calm and centered."

The Heart of the Matter

In five sentences or less, summarize the key ideas, the essence, of Chapter 22: Denials and Affirmations.

_____

_____

_____

_____

_____

Putting It Into Practice

• Make a list of your most frustrating emotions/fears. Create five denials and five replacement affirmations of Truth. Repeat these several times throughout the day, every day for 30 days. Become aware of the difference this makes in how you think and feel.

• Employ what we call the "Fillmore Challenge." The following statement is attributed to both Charles and Myrtle, depending on the source, but essentially what they said was this: *"Never make an assertion, no matter how true it may look on the surface, that you do not want to see manifest in your life!"* This is so powerful! Something as simple as the statement "I'm having a bad hair day" is something you do not want to see manifest—so why would you give power to it through your words? Set a goal of moving through an entire day without saying anything you do not want to see manifest in your life. This is an incredibly inspiring adventure—and one that will serve you well!

CHAPTER TWENTY-THREE

CREATION

Why Is This Important?

This chapter is a general overview of the process by which we bring everything into existence. While all of the basic ideas have already been reviewed, it is important for us to know we, in Truth, are creators. We are always creating, whether it is in our own minds or in the outer realm. We are the choosers. We choose what ideas and thoughts we move from the realm of consciousness to the realm of physicality.

What's in It for Me?

Knowing the overall process by which you create helps you gain more conscious control over your inner and outer experiences. You can now more consciously create your inner world of awareness as well as the outer realm of form. Your starting point is always Divine Mind and Divine Ideas. These Divine Ideas are rarely perceived in their purity because collective and individual consciousness are coloring and modifying the Divine Ideas. You use the resultant thoughts and feelings to manifest, first in consciousness and then in outer form. You more effectively create—manifest—demonstrate—when you know you are always using the Divine Process of Divine Order: Mind-Idea-Expression/mind-idea-expression.

Application Examples

Whatever the situation, whether it is to resolve a problem or to create something new, the process is the same.

1. Let's say you want to write a book. The creation of this book begins as a glimmer of an idea, which you enlarge and amplify over time. Thoughts held with feeling in mind produce after their kind. As you think about the idea, related ideas and thoughts arise in your conscious awareness. You are more excited about some than others; your feeling nature is more engaged with some than others. Mind-idea-expression is in play; it always is. Expression is happening first in consciousness. As you continue to flesh out the ideas, you write them down, organize them and, eventually, end up with a book.

2. Perhaps you want to create a tapestry for your living room wall. First of all, the idea of creating a tapestry might seem to be based on your senses (sense consciousness, your sensing function) since you have admired tapestries seen in various places. However, since

everything in the relative realm is ultimately based on Divine Ideas, the concept of a tapestry is based on a Divine Idea. As you reflect on creating the tapestry, more ideas and thoughts arise. You might even get an "inspired idea" after investing time in your daily meditation. As you reflect on this idea you will get more and more ideas and thoughts. You will have stronger feelings about some than others. Your selection of what the tapestry will look like is based on what you think and feel. You are actively using Mind-Idea-Expression/mind-idea-expression to first create the tapestry in your mind (your consciousness). Over time, you begin to bring the tapestry you have created in your mind into physical reality.

The Heart of the Matter

In five sentences or less, summarize the key ideas, the essence, of Chapter 23: Creation.

_____

_____

_____

_____

_____

Putting It Into Practice

- Look around your home or office. Choose five items that are particularly meaningful to you. For each item, identify a Divine Idea underwriting it and reflect on three other ways that same Divine Idea could have manifested.

- Think of your favorite hobby or passion. How do you use mind-idea-expression to experience that hobby/passion and create activities associated with it?

CHAPTER TWENTY-FOUR

THE TWELVE POWERS

AND

CHAPTER TWENTY-FIVE

DEVELOPING THE TWELVE POWERS

Why Is This Important?

The two chapters on the Twelve Powers present a framework for mastering the art of living, as well as practical tools to enhance and elevate our level of consciousness. Each Power is an ability, faculty or capacity we can call on, and when we use the Powers in an optimum and balanced way, we regenerate our Christ Consciousness. We manifest the Christ we already are.

Here is a quick review of the Twelve Powers:

Power	Color	Location in Body	Description
Faith	Royal Blue	Pineal Gland	Ability to believe with confidence, have conviction
Strength	Spring Green	Small of Back	Ability to endure, stay the course, persist, persevere
Wisdom	Yellow	Solar Plexus	Ability to evaluate, discern, appraise, apply what you know
Love	Pink	Back of Heart	Ability to harmonize, unify, attract
Dominion (Power)	Purple	Root of Tongue	Ability to master, dominate, control
Imagination	Light Blue	Between the Eyes	Ability to image, envision, dream, conceptualize
Understanding	Gold	Front Brain	Ability to know, perceive
Will	Silver	Front Brain	Ability to choose, decide, lead
Order	Olive Green	Back of Navel	Ability to organize, balance, sequence

Power	Color	Location in Body	Description
Zeal	Orange	Brain Stem	Ability to be enthusiastic and passionate, to start, to motivate
Elimination	Russet	Lower Intestinal Region	Ability to release, remove, deny, let go
Life	Red	Reproductive Center	Ability to energize, vitalize, enliven, be whole and healthy

You can find more detailed information about the Twelve Powers in Chapters 24 and 25 of *Heart-Centered Metaphysics*.

What's in It for Me?

These Powers are for regenerating Christ Consciousness! Once you learn you are "hardwired" with these Twelve Powers/Abilities and are already using them unconsciously, you can begin drawing on them more consciously. The more you learn about the Powers and practice employing them in your everyday life, the more you will deliberately choose to use them to improve your decisions and respond in healthier ways to every situation. You can become a better person and eventually, hopefully sooner than later, be the Christ you already are.

Application Examples

There are several ways to apply, employ and elevate these Powers in your life. Be sure to review the detailed discussion in Chapter 25, Section T, of *Heart-Centered Metaphysics* for more information.

1. As you become aware of all Twelve Powers/Abilities and truly familiar with how they operate, you observe how you use them in your everyday life. You move your awareness of how you are already using each of the Powers from a subconscious or unconscious way to a more conscious level. You begin using the Powers consciously, even if it is still from more of an ego/personality level.

   For example, as you go about your day, you have a really supportive and uplifting interaction with a co-worker. As you reflect back over the experience, you realize you used the Power of Judgment to positively evaluate your co-worker. You were able to see the Christ, her True Nature, in place of focusing on the personality. You used the Power of Will to make that choice, as well as selecting how to respond to her.

2. You consciously decide which Powers/Abilities to bring into play to have the most effective meeting or social event possible. For example, a big Thanksgiving family dinner is coming up, and while it is generally a relaxed and happy event, there are sometimes uncomfortable moments, especially if the drinking gets out of control. You know you get argumentative if you have too much to drink. So you make a conscious choice to focus on the Powers of Love, Understanding, Judgment and Will:

-   Love (the Ability to Desire) is selected because you desire a harmonious and relaxed Thanksgiving holiday with your family.

-   Understanding (the Ability to Know) is used with Judgment (the Ability to Discern and Evaluate) so you can evaluate how much to drink as well as to monitor how you feel.

-   Will (the Ability to choose) is important for making wise choices based on what is discerned.

The Heart of the Matter

In five sentences or less, summarize the key ideas, the essence, of Chapter 24: The Twelve Powers and Chapter 25: Developing the Twelve Powers.

_____

_____

_____

_____

_____

Putting It Into Practice

-   Focus on a specific Power during your meditation time. See how many ways you can bring that focus to your meditation, activating and strengthening it.

-   Choose to use a "Power of the Day" as you go about your regular activities. Keep that Power in your conscious awareness, checking out how you are using it throughout your day, as well as investing time in retrospection at the end of your day, critiquing your effectiveness with using the Power at your highest, most elevated level.

- After a meeting or social event, use the Power of Judgment to critique how it went. Ask yourself questions such as:
  - Did I effectively engage the Powers as I had intended prior to the event?
  - What other Powers could I have engaged once the event was in progress?
  - Was I informing the Powers primarily from my ego/personality?
  - Was I at least attempting to inform their use from a higher level of consciousness?

- At the end of your day, reflect on what Powers you have used and from what level of consciousness. Can you identify how you have used all Twelve Powers? If so, which ones and when? The intent is to become very conscious of the Powers so that you more actively use them every day.

Section 4:

Proving the Truth We Know

CHAPTER TWENTY-SIX

THE KINGDOM OF HEAVEN— THE FOURTH DIMENSION

Why Is This Important?

This chapter focuses on the metaphysical difference between the Kingdom of God (the Absolute) and the Kingdom of Heaven (the amount of the Kingdom of God we are actually aware of and use). This knowledge forms a basis for evaluating how we are doing on our spiritual journey, the journey in consciousness.

This chapter also provides a general framework for understanding how we move amorphous, unformed Divine Ideas from the Absolute Realm to the relative realm, from the infinite to the finite, from the unformed to the formed.

What's in It for Me?

In this chapter, you get a useful framework for discerning and understanding where you are in your progress and process of being the Christ you already are. The chapter also gives you a general understanding of a flow of consciousness from the unformed to the formed, Absolute to the relative.

Application Examples

This chapter is informational in nature and therefore application is indirect. The information in this chapter gives philosophical support to many of the previous chapters, especially those dealing with manifestation and demonstration. Here are a few application examples to help you make the information more practical:

1. You notice how an idea or thought emerges into your awareness from the amorphous, unformed, infinite field of potential and possibility that we also call the Absolute. You then notice how you give an idea or thought more and more form and shape in consciousness. In a sense, this happens when you limit the idea and thought based on your evaluation of them, and the choices you make based on those evaluations. For example, Beauty is a Divine Idea in the Absolute. It is nonspecific and amorphous; in the relative, it manifests as something visible, measurable and specific, such as a garden, a painting or a crystal vase.

2. You notice just what Divine Ideas you are aware of as well as set an intention to learn of more. For example, as you think about Beauty as a Divine Idea, you begin to look for examples in the relative of Beauty manifested. The more you know, the more you can be and apply.

The Heart of the Matter

In five sentences or less, summarize the key ideas, the essence, of Chapter 26: The Kingdom of Heaven—The Fourth Dimension.

_____

_____

_____

_____

_____

_____

Putting It Into Practice

• We call this technique "reverse engineering." Go visit a favorite landscaped area (such as a park, garden, your own backyard). Just devote time observing the area. Now, step by step, work backward by identifying how this area was created.

• There are several Divine Ideas that underwrite the landscaped area you are viewing. Identify some of them and how each Idea is manifested in the landscape.

CHAPTER TWENTY-SEVEN

THE CREATIVE PROCESS

Why Is This important?

This chapter explores an expanded form of Cause and Effect as well as Divine Order, Mind-Idea-Expression/mind-idea-expression. It also provides a wonderful tool based on the metaphysical interpretation of Genesis 1. The first seven days of creation metaphysically reflect the creative process in consciousness that precedes physical manifestation/demonstration.

What's in It for Me?

You have one more way to deliberately manifest, first in consciousness and then into form. Keep in mind that this seven-step process is not used in isolation from the other concepts and practical tools presented in *Heart-Centered Metaphysics*; it is simply another structure with which to work. You probably already noticed that some of the Twelve Powers make up this process. It is an example of how the Twelve Powers enter into the flow of consciousness presented in the previous chapter.

If you are having some difficulty demonstrating/manifesting in your life, you can very consciously use this seven-step process to make what you want more "concrete" in your consciousness. Then you would use a similar process to take what you have created in consciousness and move it into physicality. This process is based on Genesis, Chapter 2 and part of Chapter 3. [You can explore this in more detail by taking the Spiritual Education and Enrichment Class entitled "The Creative Process."]

Application Examples

You want to experience more prosperity in your life. While you affirm and claim "I am Christ; I am prosperity and abundance," you employ the following process:

1st Day: Light/ Illumination – Understanding

> You become still and invest time in meditation. Either during your meditation time or some time later, you have a "hint," a kind of knowing, an idea; the idea is to go back to school to get your master's degree. At first it seems more like something on the fringes of your waking consciousness.

2nd Day: Firmament – Faith

> You begin to focus on this idea, believing it is possible. By focusing on it, you make it more firm in your consciousness.

What we focus on in consciousness, grows in consciousness. Thoughts held with feeling in mind produce after their kind.

3rd Day: Dry Land – Imagination

You start to use your Power of Imagination to visualize and conceptualize all that you need to do to get the degree. You also imagine what your life is like once you get the degree. You begin to do your research on what it will take.

4th Day: Sun and the Moon – Understanding and Will

As you do your research, you begin to know and understand more and more about what it will take to get the degree. You use your Power of Will to make choices based on what you understand, what you know. For example, you gain a lot of information about the exact master's degree program, which schools offer it in your area, the financial expense, and the amount of time the program requires.

5th Day: Fish and Fowl – Judgment

Judgment is used to sort, evaluate and compare choices.

6th Day: Bringing Forth After Their kind – Love and Wisdom

Love and Wisdom are the Powers employed for discerning what you desire, what your end goal is, and how you are going to go about it.

7th Day: Rest – Sabbath

You rest a while, but this is not a passive resting. It is resting in the realization and assurance that you will manifest this degree. Sabbath is also based on faith. It is a mental resting and not necessarily a physical resting. All is prepared in consciousness for outer manifestation. Obviously, action must follow in order to bring the idea to full fruition.

Reminder: As you work with the Creative Process, you will notice it uses some but not all of the Twelve Powers.

The Heart of the Matter

In five sentences or less, summarize the key ideas, the essence, of Chapter 27: The Creative Process.

_____

_____

_____

_____

_____

_____

Putting It Into Practice

• Choose something you have created. (This can be anything you have made, some kind of recipe you created, artwork, poetry or journal entries, dance choreography, or a Play-Doh sculpture.) Take each of the steps of the Creative Process and identify how you employed them in your creation.

• Think of an idea you have that you would like to bring into manifestation. Using the steps of the Creative Process, write a plan of action to move the idea into actualization.

CHAPTER TWENTY-EIGHT

STUMBLING BLOCKS AND KEYS TO DEMONSTRATION

Why Is This Important?

This chapter presents possible stumbling blocks to demonstration, along with techniques to overcome them and a grand review/overview of the Principles, Ideas/ideas, concepts and practical tools presented in *Heart-Centered Metaphysics*.

What's in It for Me?

This is the place to identify the specific stumbling blocks to your manifestations. This is also where you find the tools for overcoming those stumbling blocks.

This chapter is a generic "go-to" resource when you want a reminder about the Principles, Ideas/ideas, concepts and practical tools you can use to change your consciousness and/or manifest something in the relative realm. We define stumbling blocks as self-imposed limitations or reactions to external events or feelings. If you need more than this tickler, you can always refer back to the previous chapters in *Heart-Centered Metaphysics*.

The key to remember is this: While stumbling blocks and obstacles may seem to be in the outer realm, they are primarily rooted in consciousness as thoughts and feelings.

Application Examples

1. You want to go back to school but feel you can't because your life is already full with work and family obligations. While these issues are in the outer realm, you realize your attitude and mindset about these conditions are the real obstacles; these are in your consciousness. After all, there are plenty of people who are in the exact same position and still find a way to go back to school. Since the obstacles are in consciousness, the solution must also be in consciousness. You call on Zeal and Dominion through meditation, affirmative prayer, denials and affirmations, to overcome your thoughts and feelings about these obstacles. This moves you to a place where you can begin to take action toward going back to school.

2. When you find yourself in fear of not being able to meet your bills, you use joy to counteract the fear, so your denials and affirmations are more effective. You choose to sing a happy tune or a joy song,

recognizing that doing this is much like using noise-cancelling headphones that cancel out ambient sounds so you can better enjoy your music. By shifting from a fear-based attitude that keeps you grounded in the problem, you are able to shift into a more positive, joyful attitude that opens the way for solutions to appear.

The Heart of the Matter

This is a large summary chapter involving a variety of stumbling blocks to demonstration, ways to overcome them, and key ideas for manifestation. Summarize five key ideas that were most valuable to you as you read Chapter 28: Stumbling Blocks and Keys to Demonstration.

_____

_____

_____

_____

_____

_____

Putting It Into Practice

- For each of the following situations, identify what you believe to be the primary stumbling block: fear, attachment, resistance or unforgiveness. For each situation, create a plan of action to overcome the stumbling block and move toward manifestation. We will be calling each plan of action a "prescription" and use the medical symbol "Rx" to represent it.

    a. You have made the decision to deepen your spiritual practice by having a daily time for meditation using Centering Prayer. As you begin doing this, you find your "monkey mind thoughts" are interfering. The more you try to control and quiet them, the louder and more annoying they become. You are ready to conclude that Centering Prayer is not a technique that works for you.

    STUMBLING BLOCK: _____

    Rx: _____

    _____

    b. You want to apply for a job that would be a great step up for you, both financially and professionally. As you begin to complete the application, you realize your qualifications aren't strong enough and believe you could never be selected. You panic at the thought of the interview, which includes a presentation to an interview team. You are ready to tear up the application and remain in the comfortable, safe, unfulfilling job you now have.

STUMBLING BLOCK: _____

Rx: _____

_____

c. A few years ago, you were devastated when your partner ended your relationship. You still harbor feelings of anger, hurt and resentment and continue to replay the incident in your mind, formulating all kinds of judgments about your former partner and the way in which the breakup happened. You share your "sad story" whenever you can, relishing the negative feelings and scenarios you can relate. The blame is all on your former partner and the focus is on what was done "to" you. As you begin a new relationship with someone different, you find yourself bringing up all the old stories, feeling the pain all over again.

STUMBLING BLOCK: _____

Rx: _____

_____

d. You have found the "perfect house" you want to purchase. You know this is *the* house for you! You find yourself feeling nervous and worried about getting your current house sold and having your offer for the "perfect house" accepted so you will be able to buy that "perfect house."

STUMBLING BLOCK: _____

Rx: _____

_____

• Select some area of your life where you feel like you are stuck and it appears the Principles are not working in terms of manifesting the results you desire. Write a paragraph summarizing the situation. Then determine which internal stumbling blocks are at work, and create an Rx for yourself. Next—get busy putting your prescription into practice!

CHAPTER TWENTY-NINE

METAPHYSICAL BASIS FOR WHOLENESS AND HEALTH

Why Is This Important?

The metaphysical basis of health is important in any demonstration of wholeness: with physical health, it begins with putting God (the Absolute Realm of God consisting of Divine Ideas, Principles and Laws) first. This includes the Principle of Wholeness and the Divine Idea of Life, as well as the Perfect Body Idea, the Perfect Pattern.

As we think about our physical bodies, it is not God but the outer expression of our own consciousness (consisting of collective and individual beliefs) that colors and modifies the Perfect Body Idea. Our consciousness limits Wholeness, the Divine Idea of Life, and Perfect Body Idea (the Perfect Pattern in God-Mind).

Ultimately, to quote Chapter 33, section C, of *Heart-Centered Metaphysics*, "We must come to the realization that we are not bodies, and we are not matter or simply the conscious and subconscious minds; we are Spirit, Christ, Oneness, Beingness, Divine Mind."

What's in It for Me?

Once you realize God is not directly manifesting your physical body, you can take more responsibility for your body. What you believe about your body is reflected in your physical body. This happens as all things happen, through the Law of Mind Action and the orderly process of Divine Order: Mind-Idea-Expression/mind-idea-expression. Realizing Wholeness is your fundamental reality in Consciousness, you can now begin working on your own consciousness, focusing more on how your innate Wholeness demonstrates rewards in your physical body. You can actively begin using the Powers of Life, Love, Wisdom, Understanding and Will to manifest a whole and healthy body.

With the realization you have a body but are so much more than simply a body, you free yourself of the attachment to defining who you are simply by your body.

Application Examples

1. You believe God created your body. You also believe you are overweight because your entire family is overweight. When you put these two beliefs against each other, you realize how they contra-

dict each other. On one hand, you think God literally created your body; on the other, you believe you inherited a body that will "naturally" be overweight. These are the conclusions flowing out from these beliefs:

A. God created your body and you are stuck with it. There is nothing you can do about it.

B. You will be overweight no matter what you do because you inherited this condition. There is nothing you can do about it.

Both beliefs result in an unnecessary sense of powerlessness, which in turn leads to a kind of apathy. You might say to yourself, "It doesn't matter what I do, God created me this way." Or, "It doesn't matter what I eat or no matter how much I exercise, I will be overweight because I inherited this!" You become a classic couch potato!

Even though the solution to each of these beliefs is essentially the same, let's look at them individually.

• If you believe God created your body, you will believe you are stuck with your body as is. Fillmore said the body is "... the outer expression of consciousness; the precipitation of the thinking part of man" (*The Revealing Word* by Charles Fillmore, Unity Books). When you realize God is not directly manifesting your body, but that in the Absolute Realm there is simply the Perfect Body Idea, you begin to regain your power. You realize the Perfect Body Idea is in Divine Mind (God) and what you do with the Perfect Body Idea is determined by your own consciousness. It is the collective and individual beliefs you hold in your own consciousness that are modifying and coloring the originating Divine Idea of body. You can begin identifying and disempowering the limiting beliefs with denials and claim the Truth with affirmations. As you change and recondition your consciousness, there is the greater possibility of having the body you want. By investing time in prayer and meditation, clearing your consciousness of all negative thinking and beliefs regarding your weight, and affirming whatever Truth arises into your awareness, you reclaim your power and affect change. And, most important, you take action by changing your diet and increasing your exercise.

• If you believe you inherited a body that will be overweight, you will also believe you can do nothing about it. You can overcome this belief just as Myrtle Fillmore overcame her beliefs related to inherited illness. She disempowered the belief and asked her body to forgive her for holding such beliefs. Remember, it took Myrtle two years; you will want to call on your Power of Strength to stay the course. Even if you did inherit a gene or some combination of genes that impact weight, this still does not guarantee you will be overweight. Once upon a time, scientists believed that genes were absolutely determinant and could not change, but we know differently now. Genes do not absolutely determine outcome; further, we know environmental conditions can change genes. Since genes are of the relative realm, you have dominion over them. Because your True Identity is Divine, consisting of Divine Ideas in Divine Mind, you have the power to either change your genetics or not experience consequences from your current genetic makeup. The process is exactly the same as above. You use the power of mind. Here is what you do:

    a.   Invest time in prayer and meditation.

    b.   Use denials: Clear your consciousness of all negative thinking and beliefs regarding your weight.

    c.   Use affirmations: Affirm whatever Truth arises into your awareness.

    d.   And, of key importance, take action! Change your diet and exercise your body.

2.   Any physical illness is, at least in part, a reflection of consciousness. You can change your consciousness and thereby change the condition of your body. If you are prone to negative thinking, this will set up a bodily environment more susceptible to disease. You overcome the negative thinking by becoming aware of it, using denials to disempower and eliminate error thoughts, and then affirm and claim the Truth. The Truth you claim includes the Perfect Body Idea, your innate Wholeness and the Twelve Powers, especially Life, Love, Wisdom, Understanding, Will and Elimination. Essentially, you want to set up a positive mental environment that will then outpicture as a body that is less susceptible to illness. This also results in a body able to return to its innate wholeness and health more quickly.

The Heart of the Matter

In five sentences or less, summarize the key ideas, the essence, of Chapter 29: Metaphysical Basis for Wholeness and Health.

_____

_____

_____

_____

_____

Putting It Into Practice

- Journal about your personal beliefs related to the condition of your physical body. Now reflect on what the perfect Body Idea might be in Divine Mind. Compare and contrast the two. Notice any stumbling blocks to attaining the body you desire.

- Design a poster that captures the essence of your "Perfect Body Idea Credo." This poster can include visuals that reflect and inspire you, as well as denials and affirmative statements that capture the Truth of the Perfect Body Idea manifesting as you. Use the Perfect Body Idea Credo as a daily reminder of the power you have to manifest your wholeness and health.

CHAPTER THIRTY

STUMBLING BLOCKS AND KEYS TO DEMONSTRATING LIFE, WHOLENESS AND HEALTH

Why Is This Important?

Like Chapter 28, this is an overview chapter, as well as a go-to chapter if you are looking for help to manifest and experience more day-to-day health and wholeness.

What's in It for Me?

This is the chapter you consult to manifest wholeness and health, whether you wish to be healthier and more whole, or to overcome some appearance of illness or sickness.

Application Example:

You believe you are overweight and out of shape, and you want to lose 50 pounds and get in shape to run a marathon. However, you realize you are still overeating and making excuses to avoid exercise. You invest time in meditation and journaling to discover what is going on in consciousness that is blocking your success.

First, you clearly come to terms with your attachment to the specific outcome: being a specific weight and looking a certain way. Next, you realize you must deal with your resistance to exercise and healthy eating. You become aware your real resistance is connected to a fear of failure: failure to complete the marathon.

The solution is to treat the fear by realizing your consciousness is greater than any fear of failure. You now claim, "I am Christ, whole, perfect and successful."

The Heart of the Matter

This is a large summary chapter involving a variety of stumbling blocks to demonstrating life, wholeness and health, ways to overcome those stumbling blocks and key ideas for manifestation. Summarize five key ideas that were most valuable to you as you read Chapter 30: Stumbling Blocks and Keys to Demonstrating Life, Wholeness and Health.

_____

_____

_____

_____

_____

_____

Putting It Into Practice

• Create a scenario that represents how each of the following stumbling blocks might play out in the relative realm, related to *your* wholeness and health. Then write a prescription that would help you overcome that particular stumbling block and manifest your wholeness and health.

    a. Fear and the Negative Side

    b. Attachment

    c. Resistance

    d. Unforgiveness

CHAPTER THIRTY-ONE

METAPHYSICAL BASIS FOR PROSPERITY

Why Is This Important?

We must not focus on possessions and the accumulation of physical wealth as the measure of prosperity. Prosperity is a state of consciousness, and it is about unfolding more and more of our innate Divine Nature, Christ.

Divine Substance is not matter and yet is the "matrix" that makes all form possible. Ultimately our supply lies in the Divine Ideas we use to manifest our lives based on our current level of consciousness.

When we focus on money and other outer forms of prosperity, we are focusing on effect instead of cause. It is like pointing to the movement of the trees and calling it the wind. The movement of the trees is an effect of the wind; the wind is the cause. Money and outer forms of prosperity are but the symbols or effects of Divine Ideas. Therefore, we must take an inner approach to prosperity—and how we use the effects of prosperity.

It is important to give freely and receive freely. Giving and receiving are two aspects of the same law of increase. Tithing is one way we give of what we have received.

What's in It for Me?

When you take the inner approach to prosperity, your life will have much more meaning. Instead of defining yourself by what you have, you now define your life by what (Christ Consciousness) you are. As in all Spiritual Truth, it begins in Divine Mind, God. You more easily demonstrate prosperity in the outer realm when your awareness of your inner realm is full and rich.

You more consciously use Divine Ideas from higher levels of consciousness, realizing that all ideas, whether Divine or relative, by their nature express abundance, prosperity. This is because ideas:

- Can never be used up.
- Can be utilized in an infinite number of ways.
- Grow when they are shared with others.

Application Example

You realize that for years and years you have been carrying the belief that there is never enough. In fact, you cannot remember a time when you did not believe this. While you certainly can spew out a whole litany of examples when you thought you did not have enough, you realize—when you are honest with yourself—that you have actually had a pretty good life. You recognize this belief is more about how you spur yourself to have more stuff than about not really having what you need. You decide to invest a bit more time in meditation and prayer. As you do, you come to know—really know—stuff only provides fleeting satisfaction. You discover it is the inner work and growth that truly satisfy. You understand it has always been an inside job; your worth is tied to what you are and not so much to who you are and what you have.

You decide you no longer want your old belief that there is never enough, nor do you want the associated feelings it brings, so you formulate a denial to have available each and every time you are aware of having or reactivating this belief. You also have an affirmation ready to use immediately after the denial. The denial is something like, "I give no power to and dissolve the belief there is never enough." You claim, "I am Christ; I am prosperity and abundance. I demonstrate it moment to moment."

The Heart of the Matter

In five sentences or less, summarize the key ideas, the essence, of Chapter 31: Metaphysical Basis for Prosperity.

_____

_____

_____

_____

_____

Putting It Into Practice

• For an entire week, focus on ways you can and do give. This could include giving money, assistance or help, items that are no longer serving you, etc. Keep track in your journal of how this giving impacts you.

• During the course of a day, every time you spend money, take a moment to focus on the concept that this money is a symbol that represents invisible, unlimited, ever-present Mind Substance. Notice how this awareness affects your thoughts and attitudes about money and prosperity, and keep track of your experiences in your journal. If you don't notice an appreciable effect in just one day, consider using this practice for a number of days and identify when you begin to notice a change in consciousness about money and prosperity.

- For the next month, set the intention that whenever you tithe or give a love offering, you will pause and remember that this is one way you are putting God first in your life. By donating where you receive your spiritual good, you are creating an outer symbol of the inner knowing there is only One Power and One Presence.

STUMBLING BLOCKS AND KEYS TO DEMONSTRATING PROSPERITY

Why Is This Important?

This is an overview chapter; a go-to chapter for help in manifesting and experiencing more day-to-day prosperity, both inner and outer.

What's in It for Me?

This is the chapter you consult to manifest inner and outer prosperity.

Application Example

A year ago you decided to sell your house and purchase a new one. You need to sell your current home in order to have the down payment, and you are getting frustrated because your current house has not yet sold. Until now, you have been focused on changes in the physical realm in order to sell the house, such as changing realtors, lowering the price, and repainting rooms. You begin to wonder if there might be something in your consciousness that is holding you back. You do some meditation and journaling, and realize you have a fear of lack due to the larger mortgage payment for the new home. You are attached to keeping your current home because it is the home in which you raised your children and where your grandchildren come to play; and you are resistant to buying the new home because of all the work that is involved in moving. Once you recognize these stumbling blocks, you are able to take steps to eliminate them. For example:

- **Fear:** You affirm the Truth of One Power and One Presence and unlimited supply. You also run the numbers to reassure yourself that you do have enough to handle the new mortgage payment.

- **Attachment:** You realize you will always have your memories in your consciousness, and you have the ability to create new memories wherever you are living.

- **Resistance:** You realize your resistance to moving has to do with the belief that you are not as young as you used to be. You use denials to disempower this belief, and you claim the Truth by affirming your vitality, your enthusiasm and your strength.

To strengthen your consciousness throughout this process, you set the intention to meditate and pray daily. You carry a list of the Twelve Powers with you as a reminder to use these Powers in the most productive way in order to raise your consciousness and sell your house.

The Heart of the Matter

This is a large summary chapter involving a variety of stumbling blocks to demonstrating prosperity, ways to overcome them, and key ideas for manifestation. Summarize five key ideas that were most valuable to you as you read Chapter 32: Stumbling Blocks and Keys to Demonstrating Prosperity.

_____

_____

_____

_____

_____

Putting It Into Practice

- Quickly, without any judgment or thought, complete the following statement in 10 different ways. Use whatever pops into your mind.

When it comes to the topic of prosperity, I believe . . .

1. _____
2. _____
3. _____
4. _____
5. _____
6. _____
7. _____
8. _____
9. _____
10. _____

- Now go back and review each belief statement you wrote. Determine if the statement comes from error consciousness or from Truth. For those that come from error, create a denial and a powerful affirmation you can use to expunge the error thought and implant Truth.

CHAPTER THIRTY-THREE

CREATING A METAPHYSICAL DEMONSTRATION PLAN

Why Is This Important?

A well-known saying goes like this: "If you fail to plan, you plan to fail." A concrete and measurable metaphysical demonstration plan is *the* most direct way to get what you want. When we are familiar with Divine Ideas, Divine Laws and Principles, we use them more consciously and more deliberately. Where demonstration may have seemed haphazard in the past, now we can clearly define a path forward.

What's in It for Me?

With this chapter, you have a clear procedure for creating a plan to change your consciousness, change your circumstances, and manifest in the outer realm.

Your primary work always begins in consciousness. The generalized coherent process and plan presented in this chapter are simply a guide. Feel free to modify and adjust them to fit your needs. As stated in *Heart-Centered Metaphysics*:

> While this material [in Chapter 33] will be fairly comprehensive, it is not intended to cover and include every practical idea presented in the book. This chapter is simply intended as a tool and starting point to help you apply these magnificent Principles, beliefs and ideas to your everyday life, whether it is in meeting a challenge or in wanting to create something new in your life (Introduction to Chapter 33).

> Use these questions as a way to direct your process of creating a plan to handle a situation and/or create more good in your life. Please keep in mind that not all the questions and points may be applicable to your situation. In his book, *The Universe Is Calling*, Eric Butterworth said that "it is not about making things right but seeing things rightly." In every situation, we put our Christ Nature first, expecting illumination and Understanding. Change must be first in consciousness or other sins (errors) will surely arise. Change in the outer world of the senses then may follow. The most important change we can make is the change from the limitations of sense consciousness and personal consciousness to unlim-

ited Christ Consciousness. We must come to the realization that we are not bodies, and we are not matter or simply the conscious and subconscious minds; we are Spirit, Christ, Oneness, Beingness, Divine Mind (Section 33C, Metaphysical Implementation Process and Plan).

Application Example

For the sake of continuity and consistency, let's revisit the example of the person who is overweight and believes she inherited this condition: "It's in my genetic make-up." For simplicity, this will be written in the first person, from the perspective of the woman holding the belief.

1. What is the situation, problem, challenge or need? (Describe)

I am overweight. My parents and my grandparents are all overweight. I am stuck and doomed with being overweight. I am tired all the time, and I have not had a date in years.

2. What do I hold in my mind that contributes to the situation, problem, challenge or need?

Well, I think there is nothing I can do about it.

a. How does this "serve" me? (What benefit do I think I am getting from this?)

If I inherited this kind of body, there is nothing I can do about it. So I don't have to take any responsibility for what my body looks like. I can eat anything I want and do not have to exercise. I have a built-in excuse for being overweight.

b. How is this person mirroring an aspect of myself?

As I think about this, I realize I see myself in my mother and father. Hmmm, they eat anything they want and spend most of their time sitting around watching TV. Why shouldn't I do that too?

c. Am I resisting, and if so, how? Why?

I am certainly resisting exercising in any way. I have never liked exercise. Besides, the kids in school used to laugh at me. If I go to the gym, I think people will make fun of me.

d. What am I feeling? (Chapter 18)

I feel bad. I feel frustrated and unhappy about my weight and how I am so limited by it. I am apathetic, and sometimes I get depressed and really down. I am so embarrassed by the way I look.

e. What am I thinking? (Chapter 18)

I am always thinking about my weight and how I got a bum deal when it comes to my genetic make-up. I think I am a victim of my own genes. I think there is nothing I can do about it.

f. ***What am I sensing? (Chapter 18)***

Sight—I see my fat body in the mirror and I do not like what I see. I am reminded of being overweight whenever I see a flimsy piece of furniture.

Smell—I certainly love the way some food smells! And I am certainly embarrassed to say that sometimes I perspire heavily with little exertion and then do not smell good.

Taste—Boy, oh, boy, I love the way food tastes—especially the sweet stuff!

Touch—My body feels flabby all over. Most chairs and sofas feel tight and uncomfortable, as do my clothes. I avoid flying because seats in coach feel so uncomfortable.

Sound—I certainly hear how some of the material of my clothing rubs together. I also hear people saying unkind things about my weight. And to be honest, I hear all the negative things I am saying about myself!

g. ***What am I intuiting? (Chapter 18)***

It has just been niggling at me for quite some time. It is as if a voice is saying, "You can do something about your weight." A part of me seems to know I can do something about my weight.

h. ***What are my old mental messages or beliefs about this?***

I am overweight and I will always be overweight. I am overweight because my parents are overweight. There is nothing I can do about it … yada, yada, yada. I am so tired of this worn-out story.

i. ***Can I detect any error thinking?***

Plenty. If what I have been studying in this book is correct, I have been really victimizing myself with my own error thinking. While it may be a fact that my parents are overweight, this does not mean I have to be overweight.

3. What do I know about Oneness, my Christ Nature, or Principle that can apply here? (Chapter 10)

Well, in Truth I am Christ, forever whole and perfect. There is a perfect Idea of body in Divine Mind. There are also the Twelve Powers, especially the Powers of Life, Strength, Elimination.

4. What Spiritual Law(s) can I apply to this situation and how?

Law of Mind Action, Law of Divine Order

5. What tools will help me with this situation? (Be specific.)

Practicing the Silence (meditation), Prayer, Power of the Word, Denials and Affirmations come to mind.

Silence—I will practice the Silence so I am more aware of my True Identity, trusting Divine Ideas will inspire relative ideas and thoughts useful in my losing weight.

Prayer—I will claim wholeness and health. I will actively claim the Powers I need in any given situation.

a. *How am I going to apply them?*

Denials and Affirmations—After formulating denials and affirmations I will start using them during my prayer times. I will use my mealtimes to remind myself to use them. I will deny giving any power or importance to my thoughts and beliefs about my weight. I will consciously become aware of my weight-related beliefs, thoughts and feelings. Once aware, I will formulate the denials and use them every time I am aware of those error beliefs, thoughts and feelings. For now I will use the following denials:

> *I give no power or importance to any belief about inheriting being overweight.*
>
> *I give no power to the belief I am only this body.*
>
> *I give no power to the thought I can do nothing about my weight.*
>
> *I dissolve all beliefs about inheriting a weight problem.*

I use the Power of the Word to engage specific affirmations such as:

> *I am Christ, forever whole and perfect.*
>
> *I am height and weight proportionate.*
>
> *I eat and drink in support of a healthy body.*

b. *When?*

I will do the affirmations during my morning meditation and prayer time. I use them every time I eat or want to eat. I am vigilant for any erroneous thinking. As soon as I am aware, I apply my denials and affirmations.

c. *How often?*

At least four times a day.

d. *Where?*

Wherever I happen to be at the time. Losing all these pounds is a high priority.

e. *Am I committed to doing this?*

Yes. In fact, I will ask my friend Sally to be my accountability partner. I will agree to report in on at least a weekly basis. I will figure out what I can do with ease and grace for exercise and changing my diet. I will leave little to chance.

6. Write a prayer of gratitude.

I am grateful for all the inspired ideas and thoughts from Divine Mind. I am grateful I have the strength and will to follow through on taking off this weight. I am grateful for Sally supporting me in this process.

The Heart of the Matter

List the six steps of creating a Metaphysical Demonstration Plan, as described in Chapter 33: Creating a Metaphysical Demonstration Plan.

_____

_____

_____

_____

_____

_____

Putting It Into Practice

• Using the material in *Heart-Centered Metaphysics* summarized in Chapter 33, create a Metaphysical Demonstration Plan of your own and put it into practice. For your first Metaphysical Demonstration Plan, choose something you have complete control over in your own consciousness. Don't try to swallow the big frog first. Start small and build your understanding, experience and confidence.

ANSWER KEY

Here it is—the Answer Key! Obviously, when we are talking about metaphysical principles and concepts, there is a lot of room for personal interpretation of our experiences, as well as ongoing expansion of awareness and consciousness. However, we have tried to help you in your study by providing, where appropriate, examples of answers that are on the right track. In order to make this Answer Key easy to work with, we have included the original question in italics, followed by suggested responses.

Chapter One—Metaphysics and Truth

The Heart of the Matter

Summarize this chapter in five sentences or less. Your response may include some of the following concepts:

- Metaphysics is concerned with matters that lie beyond the physical realm.
- Metaphysics deals with Ultimate Reality through the lens of the heart, rather than focusing simply on hard facts.
- Relative truth refers to the world of our senses (the world of appearances), while Absolute Truth refers to the Realm of Divine Ideas. At the level of the Absolute, Truth is universal, unchanging and complete.
- When we shift our awareness from the relative to the Absolute, we are able to change our thinking and thereby use our power of thought to manifest greater good in our lives.

Putting It Into Practice

Read each statement below and determine whether it is relative (r) or Absolute (A).

    _A_ There is no death.
    _A_ There is no sickness.
    _r_ The economy is in the tank.
    _r_ Life is not fair.
    _A_ There is only Good.
    _r_ Ice cream is yummy.
    _r_ Chocolate makes me feel better.
    _A_ There is no evil.
    _r_ Life is good.
    _A_ I am the Good.

Why is it important to distinguish between the Absolute and the relative? How does knowing this make a difference in your life?

Your answer should reflect the fact that the relative can be changed, while the Absolute is unchangeable. (Hallmarks of the relative realm: measurable, changeable, includes space and time, based on information gleaned from the senses. Hallmarks of the Absolute Realm: Not measurable, does not change, is not located in space and time, not sense-based.)

It makes a difference in your life because you have the power to change the relative things you are dissatisfied with, as well as improve upon those things you are keen on.

Look at one or more situations in your life (for example, paying the mortgage, juggling priorities, raising children, etc.). Become aware of your internal dialogue related to the situation(s) you selected. Are the statements relative or Absolute? If you realize your statements are relative, what Absolute statements could you replace them with to redefine or refocus your consciousness?

Example:

Consider this: "I do not have enough money to pay my mortgage; why am I so poor?" These are statements based on the relative, because they are changeable and measurable in time and space. Therefore, you can use an Absolute statement to refocus your consciousness, such as "In Consciousness, I am Divine Flow. I am prosperous."

As you review Chapter 1, Section D, in Heart-Centered Metaphysics *on relative existence, reflect on a project you have recently completed. Before you began the physical work on the project, you had thoughts and ideas about it. Make a list of possible First Cause Divine Ideas that stimulated your relative thoughts and ideas about the project (first effect, which then becomes the second cause).*

In the text, you read about a garden. The actual garden is manifested by your physical work. Prior to the work, there were thoughts and ideas about what a beautiful garden would look like. Some possible Divine Ideas are Beauty, Order and Peace.

Chapter Two—Life Is Consciousness

The Heart of the Matter

Summarize this chapter in five sentences or less. Your response may include some of the following concepts:

- Life is consciousness.
- Change your mind (change your thoughts and feelings), change your experience.
- In changing our own consciousness, we change our experience of the world and may change our outer lives and circumstances as well.
- Raising consciousness begins with remembering and becoming ever more aware of Oneness.
- The ultimate goal is to realize Christ Consciousness.
- We can have experiences and live from various types of consciousness as well as in various levels of consciousness—victim, victor, vessel or Verity.

Putting It Into Practice

Read each description below and determine which level of consciousness is demonstrated (victim, victor, vessel or Verity):

- Why does my line always move slowest at the supermarket? <u>victim</u>
- From my Oneness I knew what to do. <u>Verity</u>
- How can I be prosperous when the economy is so bad? <u>victim</u>
- I can overcome this situation. <u>victor</u>
- I claim the Abundance that is mine by right of Consciousness. <u>Verity</u>
- If my parents had let me take dance lessons, I would be a dancer today. <u>victim</u>
- It wasn't me. It was God working through me. <u>vessel</u>
- Even though I did not get to take dance lessons as a child, I can take them now. <u>victor</u>
- Make me an instrument. <u>vessel</u>
- While this line moves slowly, I can read the funny titles in the tabloids. <u>victor</u>
- I was called to do this. <u>vessel</u>
- I Am. <u>Verity</u>

Think of your own examples from your own experience:

A. victim consciousness—in this case, your examples will reflect something happening to you that seems to be out of your control.

B. victor consciousness—in this case, your examples will reflect that you have control and power, whether it is over your thoughts, feelings, actions, reactions or external events.

C. vessel consciousness—in this case, your examples will reflect something happening through you, seeming to come from someone or something else—aka God.

D. Verity Consciousness—in this case, your examples will reflect that you are operating from Christ Consciousness, Oneness, or God-ness.

Write your own short centering phrase to use whenever you notice that you are coming more from your ego or intellect.

Some examples of short centering phrases are:

- "Peace, be still."
- "Nothing can disturb the peace and calm of my soul."
- "I Am the Oneness. Therefore, all things are possible."

While the goal is to keep our focus always on and coming from the Oneness, sometimes it is helpful to use our senses as reminders of that Oneness:

It really doesn't matter which reminder(s) you chose. The important thing is to realize you are not saying these sensory items, in and of themselves, have power over you. You are saying that *you* are deciding that these will be sensory reminders of Oneness.

Chapter Three—Self-Knowledge

The Heart of the Matter

Summarize this chapter in five sentences or less. Your response may include some of the following concepts:

- Each of us has an inherent ability to know Truth and be Truth—Christ Consciousness.
- Self-knowledge gleaned through self-observation and awareness helps build consciousness.
- Self-acceptance prevents self-condemnation during self-observation.
- The ultimate goal is spiritual unfoldment and knowing Oneness so each of us can fully be the Christ we already are in the Absolute.
- While we may seem to have many selves or many "whos," the Truth is each of us is the totality of Christ or Christ Consciousness.

Putting It Into Practice

Make a list of what you know for sure about yourself. Also, indicate whether it is relative or Absolute and why.

An example would be:

- A mother (relative)
- A dancer (relative)
- The I AM (Absolute)
- A physician (relative)
- The Christ (Absolute)

Descartes famously said, "I think, therefore I am." Take a few moments and fill in the blank.
   "I _____, therefore I am."
   "I _____, therefore I am."
   "I _____, therefore I am."
   "I _____, therefore I am."
   "I _____, therefore I am."
Your responses will be appropriate and unique for you. Examples might be: laugh, dance, love, cook, metaphysically interpret, jog, work out, sing

Now take the list you just created and flip-flop the sentence. For example, Descartes said, "I think, therefore I am." If you flip-flopped this sentence, you would have, "I am, therefore I think." What does flip-flopping the sentences tell you about yourself from a metaphysical perspective?

Your answer should reflect that the I AM comes first and is the most important aspect. Who you think you are is an effect of and flows from how you use Divine Ideas.

Chapter Four—Evolving Spiritual Awareness, Building Christ Consciousness

The Heart of the Matter

Summarize this chapter in five sentences or less. Your response may include some of the following concepts:

- Most people eventually become aware of an innate desire to become new, to spiritually evolve an awareness of what Unity calls Christ Consciousness.
- Evolving our awareness from who we think we are to what we know we are is a step-by-step process for the vast majority of people.
- Just as Christ is the Word, the Idea that contains Ideas, so, too, is our personality simply a conglomeration of ideas and thoughts about ourselves.
- The first birth is our physical birth. The second birth describes the significant change that occurs when we commit ourselves to living more and more from the awareness of Oneness.
- Chemicalization occurs when new Spiritual Truths meet old beliefs and error thoughts sometimes resulting in physical, emotional and mental symptoms of distress.
- Crucifixion is the experience of crossing out error thinking.
- Resurrection is what happens when we have overcome error thinking or our attachment to some cherished aspect of our personality or personal life.
- Regeneration is the process that reveals and unfolds our Divinity (Christ).
- Reincarnation is a makeshift process by which humankind experiences successive lives for the purpose of soul unfoldment until we individually and collectively awaken to the full realization of the Reality of Oneness.

Putting It Into Practice

"Born Again"—As you reflect back on your life, within each decade pinpoint key experiences or "aha!" moments you would now identify as a growing awareness of Oneness.

Notice how you changed as a result of these experiences.

Examples would be:

Ages 1-10:   A key experience for me was starting first grade. Looking back, I realize this was a moment when I began to see myself as a separate individual with my own interests, my own personality and my own ways of doing things. I could assert myself, and my actions had an impact on others.

Ages 20-30:   I went through a divorce, which was one of the toughest decisions I ever made. It went against the values of my family of origin, but it was something I felt very strongly I needed to do for me. This stands out as one of the critical moments of my life because it is the first time I recall going against what I knew everyone else expected me to do. This prepared the way for my later decision to leave traditional religion and explore a different spiritual path.

[Note: If you think you experienced any change, this is what is meant by being born again from a metaphysical perspective. Being born again is not a onetime event; it is an ongoing unfoldment.]

Chemicalization—Looking back at the key experiences you identified in the last question, can you recall if you had any adverse physical reactions as you moved through them? Create a list of times you can remember when you had physical reactions (health challenges, emotional reactions, etc.) that correlate with the key experiences you identified.

Examples might be:

- When I entered first grade, I began to experience headaches for a short time. They disappeared on their own, although I remember my parents being concerned about them.

- When I went through my divorce, I remember having feelings of wanting to be in a car accident. I did not want to commit suicide, but I felt I would be better off dead than causing such hurt. This is the only time I recall ever having these deep emotional distressing thoughts. During this period, I also developed what was diagnosed as rheumatoid arthritis. The symptoms have totally disappeared now.

Resistance and Nonresistance

1. Read the following statements and notice your immediate reactions and/or push back (resistance). Then practice entering into an attitude of nonresistance to these statements.

    A.   I Am Christ.

    B.   God did not create the physical universe.

    C.   God does not fix or change us.

    D.   God is not living. God is Life.

    E.   God is not loving. God is Love.

As you do this exercise, pay close attention to things such as:

- The thoughts and inner dialogue that run through your head (for example, if I say "I Am Christ," I will go to hell for sure!).

- The physical feelings you experience (such as tightening of the stomach muscles; tension in your shoulders).

- The emotional feelings you experience (such as feelings of panic or fear).

- The question: What is it I am resisting? What if I see how it feels to believe this? How can I practice nonresistance?

2. How was your Power/Ability of Dominion in play in the exercise above?

    Your response should include something similar to the following ideas:

- The Power of Dominion is my ability to master, dominate and control.

- I use this Power at its most elevated level to make it possible to be the best Christ I can be.

- I am able to master my resistance by calling on this Power.

3. What was crucifixion in this exercise?

Your response should reflect something similar to this concept: Crucifixion was the "crossing out" of error thinking that led to my resistance to higher Truths.

4. What was resurrection in this exercise?

Your response should reflect something similar to this concept:

Resurrection is rising to a higher state of Consciousness. So in this example I resurrected to a higher level of awareness by allowing myself to be nonresistant to Truth statements.

5. What would regeneration be?

Your response should reflect something similar to this concept: Regeneration occurs when I begin to integrate these statements into my consciousness and consciously choose to live from the awareness of my Oneness rather than from sense consciousness.

Chapter Five—Our Purpose, Divine Will, Divine Plan, and Divine Guidance

The Heart of the Matter

Summarize this chapter in five sentences or less. Your response may include some of the following concepts:

- Our purpose is to realize, be and express our Divine Potential, which is Christ. This is not to say we are "here" in the relative realm for a reason. It is that we can bring "R" Reason to our being "here."

- There is no Divine Will, Divine Plan, or Divine Guidance if this means there is a God or Spirit that has predetermined your life in any way, specific shape or form.

- Divine Will is that each person ultimately reveals and expresses Christ (the composite Divine Idea). This Divine Will is generic, amorphous, nonspecific and is for everyone.

- Divine Plan is how each person decides to go about bringing forth, developing and expressing Divine Will (Christ). Our consciousness determines the direction we take in expressing the Christ, the Divine Idea that is made up of Ideas.

- Divine Guidance is the supportive "flow" of the Divine Ideal of Divine Wisdom working in concert with other Divine Ideals in Divine Mind so that each person is able to discern the road ahead and formulate the plan according to his or her level of consciousness.

Putting It Into Practice

Read the following list and determine which sentences are based on a God that determines everything and is in control versus those based on God/Divine Mind that is more a flow of Consciousness we use to make choices.

1. God told me to do it. <u>God in control</u>
2. When I remember Oneness I know what to say and do. <u>God/Divine Mind as flow of Consciousness</u>
3. God blessed me. <u>God in control</u>
4. I use my Divinity to bless and manifest. <u>God/Divine Mind as flow of Consciousness</u>
5. It is in God's hands now. <u>God in control</u>
6. God meant it to be this way. <u>God in control</u>
7. God must have a purpose or reason for this happening in my life. <u>God in control</u>
8. It's all in Divine Order. <u>God in control</u>
9. If it is going to be, it is up to me. <u>God/Divine Mind as flow of Consciousness</u>

Chapter Six—The Silence

The Heart of the Matter

Summarize this chapter in five sentences or less. Your response may include some of the following concepts:

- The Silence is perhaps the most important practice in Unity and is the starting point of becoming a heart-centered metaphysician and awakening into Christ Consciousness.
- The practice of the Silence is the meditation technique used to enter into the state of the Silence.
- The Silence is a state of total nonawareness (neither internal nor external) that "arises" as a result of the practice of the Silence meditation technique.
- The Silence is the medium in which, and from which, our True Nature, Christ, expresses.
- The Silence is a state of consciousness in which there is no experience of time, space or sensation.
- Any experience of a voice, guidance or answers is an *effect* of having been in the Silence and *does not actually occur* in the Silence.

Putting It Into Practice:

Which of these occur in the Silence?

      ___ Hearing voices

      ___ Light show

      _X_ Nothing

      ___ Warm body sensation

      _X_ No sense of time

      _X_ No sensation

      ___ Visualizations

Here is a quick and easy activity to help you discern what relaxation may feel like.

1. *Sit comfortably for a minute or two.*
2. *Notice where you are feeling any tension.*
3. *Tense and squeeze all the muscles in your body for a slow count of 10.*
4. *Scrunch your eyes, make fists, pull in your stomach, tighten your buttocks, curl your toes. We mean all your muscles! Tense! Tight!*
5. *Very slowly, begin to relax your muscles, allowing the tenseness to melt out through your feet.*
6. *Now become aware of how you feel ... relaxed and at peace.*

Obviously, what you journal about this exercise is your experience, and your responses will vary depending on your own experience. The intent of this exercise is to help you be aware of how it feels to be tense and how it feels to be relaxed. It is also a way to move from being stressed to being more relaxed in preparation for entering the Silence.

Set a timer for three minutes. Sit in a comfortable position, close your eyes and be still. Become aware of what you notice as you sit still. How are these thoughts arising in your mind? What effect do they have on sitting in the Silence?

Some examples might be: *I hear birds singing. My nose itches. I think about the project that's due tomorrow. I remember I need bananas for breakfast.* Your responses to the questions should reflect something indicating how easily and effortlessly thoughts can arise into your awareness. As you realize how easily the thoughts can arise, you can take dominion over them, lovingly "thank them for sharing," and refocus your attention on your mantra. Become aware that your mantra can arise easily and effortlessly into your consciousness, just as the distracting thoughts did.

Chapter Seven—Meditation

The Heart of the Matter

Summarize this chapter in five sentences or less. Your response may include some of the following concepts:

- In Unity, the terms *prayer* and *meditation* are often intertwined because the Five-Step Prayer Process includes meditation as the third step.
- Strictly speaking, the practice of meditation is not prayer.
- While unfortunately named, Centering Prayer is a highly recommended meditation technique for entering into the Silence. It could be thought of as a generic form of Transcendental Meditation.
- Benefits of meditation include the alleviation of constant worry, pressure and stress. Meditation can also result in more calm, peace, happiness and a sense of relaxation.
- In meditation, we work with our tendencies to be habitual beings.

Putting It Into Practice

Practice meditation for at least 30 days using the technique called Centering Prayer as outlined in the chapter. Keep in mind this is not a technique about shutting down or quieting the jabbering of the "monkey mind." The only important points about the mantra one chooses are that it:

- Be from one to seven words in length.
- Not be something that is commonly spoken outward.
- Be used and not changed no matter how much the ego/personality wants to change it! Jumping from mantra to mantra diminishes the effectiveness of the technique.

Keep a journal of your experience. Notice what effect it has on your everyday life.
   As you complete this particular exercise, the information you record in your journal will be very personal and specific to your experiences. There are no right or wrong answers here. The key is to make the time to do the practice of meditation and be aware of your experiences.

Notice all the reasons you find to not meditate. Notice what tends to get in the way. Make a list of the distractions and create strategies to work around them.
   Again, your responses here will be specific to your own experience, which is different for everyone. Some examples that other students have shared include:
   - Too busy with work-related expectations
   - Family commitments (children, partner, in-laws, outlaws, etc.)
   - Housework
   - Taking care of my pet
   - Inability to focus my attention
   - Had to work out

- Fell asleep
- Lack of personal commitment to doing it

Chapter Eight—Prayer

The Heart of the Matter

Summarize this chapter in five sentences or less. Your response may include some of the following concepts:

- Prayer is one of the most important spiritual practices.
- Unity uses affirmative prayer, which includes claiming and declaring what is already True in the Absolute Realm, or Divine Mind.
- We do not pray *to* God. We pray from the awareness of God, or our Divinity.
- Divine Ideas are the Primary Cause or Primary Basis of everything.
- Prayer is a head-and-heart, thinking-and-feeling-nature process.
- Prayer is an attitude of the heart that is more about being than doing.
- In prayer, we use our minds to lay hold of Divine Ideas (our Supply and Substance), which give rise to thoughts and ideas according to a person's level of consciousness. It is these Ideas/ideas and thoughts that we claim and declare.
- The Five-Step Prayer Process is: Relaxation, Concentration, Meditation (Silence), Realization and Thanksgiving/Gratitude.
- Relaxation refers to the relaxation of the body and the letting go of any focus on our mind chatter.
- Concentration can refer to a gentle focus on a word or phrase or a seeming prayer need.
- Meditation refers to the process or technique that results in entering the state of Silence.
- Realization is when we know that we know what is already True in Divine Mind, or the Absolute Realm.
- Thanksgiving or gratitude refers to an attitude of the heart. We are not grateful *to* God, or Divine Mind. We are simply grateful.

Putting It Into Practice

What is the difference between Affirmative Prayer and meditation?

> Your response should reflect something similar to this: Meditation refers to our entering the Silence. In prayer, we use our minds (and possibly our words) to claim and declare what we know is True in the Absolute Realm. While meditation alone contains no intentional prayer component, the process of meditation is step three of the affirmative prayer process.

Read the following sentences from prayers and determine whether the statement reflects praying to *God or reflects praying* from *the awareness of God.*

- Thank you for all the blessings You have sent. <u>To God</u>
- I am grateful for the awareness of my Oneness, knowing there is no separation. <u>From awareness of Oneness</u>

- Please send Your healing power to John as he recovers from surgery, bringing him comfort and relief. <u>To God</u>
- Dear God, help me get through this difficult time. <u>To God</u>
- The very nature of God is Love, and so I call forth that power of Love from within me, to bring harmony to my relationships. <u>From awareness of Oneness</u>
- I affirm abundant prosperity is now flowing and I am One with Divine Ideas to manifest my good. <u>From awareness of Oneness</u>

Begin a daily prayer practice, using the Five-Step Prayer Process outlined in this chapter. In your journal, record your experiences, including what you found difficult as well as positive results.

The information you capture in your journal will be very personal and will reflect your own individual experiences. It is very useful to use your journal because it helps you see trends, patterns and issues impacting your prayer life.

Chapter Nine—Praying With Others

The Heart of the Matter

Summarize this chapter in five sentences or less. Your response may include some of the following concepts:

- We pray "with" others rather than "for" others even though our common language focuses on questions like "Will you pray for me?"
- Affirmative prayer based upon Divine Ideas is used to pray with others.
- The Five-Step Prayer Process is used when praying with others.
- A seeming miracle is the result of Divine Ideas, Principles and Laws of which we are not yet aware.
- In praying with others we see beyond appearances to the Truth.
- We must not be insistent upon particular results or outcomes for individuals.
- Persistence may be required to break down the walls of resistance.

Putting It Into Practice

Select someone to be a prayer partner with you for a three-month period and schedule weekly prayer time together. (Note: After the three-month period, you may decide to continue working with your prayer partner or you may decide to find a different one. We recommend you continue the practice of having a prayer partner with whom you can create a regular prayer practice.) Keep a journal as you move through this process, recording your fears, experiences and aha's.

Your experience will be unique to you. It is important to capture your thoughts and experiences in your prayer journal, so you can go back and review them to see how you have grown as a result of this activity.

Build your awareness of the power of praying around Divine Ideas by brainstorming Divine Ideas related to the following areas:

- *Prosperity/Finance/Employment*
- *Relationships*
- *Healing*
- *Guidance*
- *Spiritual Growth*

Your responses will vary. Here are a few examples:

- Prosperity/Finance/Employment: Divine Idea of Abundance, Order
- Relationships: Divine Idea of Love, Harmony, Attraction
- Healing: Divine Idea of Life, Order, Perfection
- Guidance: Divine Idea of Oneness, Order, Understanding
- Spiritual Growth: Divine Idea of Oneness, Strength, Wisdom

Chapter Ten—Beingness, Oneness, Divine Mind

The Heart of the Matter

Summarize this chapter in five sentences or less. Your response may include some of the following concepts:

- The term *God* is a term loaded with meaning and understanding from the spiritual traditions in which we were raised.
- We cannot not truly and fully define the Divine because It is more an experience than a definition.
- God is not He or She. The best pronoun for the Divine Mind is *It*.
- Principle refers to the unlimited, unchanging, eternal Divine Mind.
- Divine Mind is Omniscience, Omnipotence and Omnipresence.
- Substance is not matter. It is the basis of all form and yet enters not into it. Substance is Divine Ideas.
- Divine Mind is the Source of our Supply, Divine Ideas.
- Divine Mind is Law or Principle in action.
- God is Love, the unifying, harmonizing and attracting Principle.
- Divine Mind is Life, the eternal activity and vitality.

Putting It Into Practice:

Think back to the God of your childhood. Journal a description of what that God was like, as best you can recall.

> Your answers will vary depending on your experience. Be sure to invest some quality time with this. You might even take some time in meditation, reflecting on your experiences related to God when you were a child.

How is the God of your childhood different from your understanding of God after reading this chapter? Journal about that. *Your responses will vary, but may include some of the following concepts:*

- There is no "God out there" in the sky.
- God is the process Itself we use to bring about effects.
- God is the unifying, harmonizing and attracting Principle.
- Divine Mind is the Source of our Supply, Divine Ideas.

Based on your new understanding of God, rewrite the Lord's Prayer.

> Again, this will be a very personal experience. The goal is to capture the essence of the Lord's Prayer while using accurate, Truth-specific wording.

Chapter Eleven—The Spiritual Universe and the Physical Universe

The Heart of the Matter

Summarize this chapter in five sentences or less. Your response may include some of the following concepts:

- One of the most commonly held beliefs about God is that God is a supernatural being who created the physical universe, including our bodies.
- Everything in the physical or manifest realm is based on Divine Ideas.
- Divine Mind creates/ideates through the action of Mind.
- The Spiritual Universe is composed of Divine Ideas.
- The body is the physical outpicturing of the thinking part of humankind, both collective and individual consciousness.
- Spiritual thoughts make a Spiritual Body; material thoughts make a material body.
- The creation as depicted in Genesis 1 is entirely spiritual.
- The "image and likeness" is the Spiritual Human or Christ.
- God created/ideated the Spiritual Universe consisting of the Divine Ideas that make the material (physical) universe possible.
- Humankind is entangled with materiality, and therefore, some manifestation is not necessarily good.
- The physical universe is the result of entanglement with our sense consciousness.
- The way out of being entangled in sense consciousness is by going into the awareness of our True Divine Nature.

Putting It Into Practice

Go outside at night and take a long look at the stars. Reflect on the following question: What does it mean at a deep level to understand that an anthropomorphic God did not create the universe?

Your responses will vary depending on your own experience. One possible response could be an awareness that I could not pray to a God out there to change the weather.

Open a new can of Play Doh. (Go ahead and smell it! We'll wait!) Spend some time creating something with your Play Doh. Once you are through, reflect on how you created this object from an idea in your mind. How is this similar to the way the universe was created?

Your responses will vary depending on your own experience but should reflect the fact that there is always first an idea in mind that is massaged and modified until there is a final result. This is true in creating with the Play Doh and is also true for the way the universe came into existence

Chapter Twelve—The Divine Paradoxes

The Heart of the Matter Your response may include some of the following concepts:

- A paradox is an assertion that may appear contradictory or opposed to common sense but is nevertheless true.
- God is Principle; God is personal. God may be realized as unfailing Principle while, at the same time, we create a very personal experience of God.
- God is Immanent; God is Transcendent. God is everywhere totally present. God seems both to be within, within consciousness, and at the same time, God is beyond this.
- God as Father; God as Mother. God is *not* Father or Mother. We assign qualities of Being related to being a father or a mother. We then identify these qualities in God or Divine Mind.
- God is Law; God is Grace. We experience Divine Mind, or God, as both unbreakable Law and unconditional Grace or Love.

Putting It Into Practice

How do you experience God in a personal way? Capture your ideas in your journal. How does this align with what you know about God from studying Chapter 10: Beingness, Oneness, Divine Mind?

> Your responses will vary depending on your own experience; however, they may reflect ideas such as this: "While I experience God as a warm and loving presence, I can also know God is simply the Principle of Love I am using to manifest that experience."

Choose one of the Four Paradoxes identified in Chapter 12 and invest one week looking for specific examples of how it shows up in your life. Capture your thoughts in your journal about the impact this paradox has on you in terms of your daily living.

> Your responses will vary depending on your own experience. An illustration might be noticing on one hand God is Law; on the other, Grace. For example, the Law of Mind Action: "I notice I hold thoughts and feelings, and they do tend to produce after their kind. At other times, I hold thoughts and feelings and they do not produce after their kind, and this happens through grace. Grace is my ability to change my mind at any time. This helps me to know that I do not always experience the full measure of the thoughts and feelings I hold."

Chapter Thirteen—The Trinity

The Heart of the Matter

Summarize this chapter in five sentences or less. Your response may include some of the following concepts:

- The Trinity (Father, Son, Holy Spirit) metaphysically represents the three primary creative aspects of Beingness.
- The three creative aspects of Beingness are Mind-Divine Idea-Expression.
- Mind is the Absolute—transcendent and immanent.
- Divine Idea is the Logos, Word or Christ—the fundamental nature underlying everything.
- Expression is our experience of the activity of Divine Mind at the point of our awareness.
- These are three ways of acknowledging Beingness.
- Mind-Idea-Expression/mind-idea-expression is always in play.

Putting It Into Practice

Make yourself a peanut butter and jelly sandwich. Using the sandwich as a metaphor, relate it to the concept of the Trinity as discussed in Chapter 13.

> Your responses may reflect ideas such as: You can experience the sandwich as a whole, or as its separate elements; like Mind-Idea-Expression, each part appears separate and distinct, yet when put together reflect something whole and unique.

As you go throughout your normal day, be on the lookout for experiences of mind-idea-expression at work.

> Your responses may include any situations where you got an idea, and then gave it a visual picture, and then brought it into manifestation. An example would be a decision to have eggs instead of oatmeal for breakfast. Even though the idea/decision to have eggs is a relative idea, it must be based on something, some Idea, in the Absolute Realm. Thus, Mind-Idea-Expression is always in play, underwriting mind-idea-expression.

Chapter Fourteen—Sin, Evil and the Devil

The Heart of the Matter

Summarize this chapter in five sentences or less. Your response may include some of the following concepts:

- The origin of sin and evil arises from humankind because we persist in thinking, feeling and believing in separation from Spirit.
- We become entangled in our sense consciousness, which gives rise to error thinking, sin and evil.
- Evil has no independent existence.
- Since we have free will, since we are free to choose, we can choose error over Truth.
- Sin and evil are the misuse and the negation of Divine Ideas.
- Satan and the devil are simply aspects of human consciousness in need of transformation.
- Temptation is a state of awareness in which we are conscious of the fact we can choose sin (error) or Truth.
- Repentance and forgiveness are about changing the mind from seeing error to seeing Truth.
- Heaven and hell are both states of consciousness.
- Heaven is a state of expanded consciousness.
- Hell is the suffering we experience when we choose to sin.

Putting It Into Practice

Go for a bicycle ride. Enjoy the excursion! While you are riding, become aware of how often you are self-correcting to stay on your desired course. When you get back home, take some time to journal about how this awareness of constantly self-correcting as you ride a bicycle is similar to how you self-correct when you "sin" (miss the mark) or are tempted to "sin."

> Your responses will vary depending on your own experience. One idea might be the tendency to gossip: "Once I decide to eliminate that habit, I become aware of it when I begin to do it. As soon as I notice I am gossiping, I stop myself and change the subject. This continual 'self-correction' helps me eliminate the habit."

Draw a picture of how you feel when you are having a "hell" experience. Now transform that picture into the way you feel when you are able to change your consciousness and turn it into a "heaven" experience. Reflect on the feelings you experienced as you did this activity—and what it tells you about your life situations.

> Your responses will vary depending on your own experience. You might add golden rays around a dark area of a picture, making you think about ways you make a conscious choice to use an experience for good, even though it may seem to be a "hell" experience from the world of appearance.

An example we thought of is the picture of an old hag (see the illustration below), that can also be viewed as a beautiful woman. It all depends on how you choose to look at it.

(Image credited to W.E. Hill, *Puck* magazine, 1915)

Chapter Fifteen—Jesus, the Christ, Jesus Christ, Christ Jesus

The Heart of the Matter

Summarize this chapter in five sentences or less. Your response may include some of the following concepts:

- Jesus is the name of a man that was born in Bethlehem and was raised in Nazareth ... the human personality and the body.
- Metaphysically, Jesus represents each person's capacity to realize Christ Potential.
- Christ is the universal Divine Idea that is made up of Ideas, the spiritual perfection inherent in Mind.
- Jesus Christ is the man who most expressed his Christ Potential.
- We metaphysically become Christ Jesus (Divine human) when we lose our personality and become the Christ.
- Christ Jesus may also be used to refer to the ascended Jesus.
- Atonement is the awareness of conscious Oneness.
- Salvation is achieved by our ongoing identification with Christ Consciousness.
- Following Jesus means following his teachings and his example.
- We must actively deny and disempower any thoughts and feelings that hinder our ability to live from Christ Consciousness.

Putting It Into Practice:

Create two separate and distinct introductions for yourself as if you were being introduced to an audience. Write the first one presenting your ego/personality. Write the second one introducing you as the Christ you already are!

> Your responses will vary depending on your own experience. For example, the one for your ego might begin "I am a 35-year-old teacher ..." The one introducing you as the Christ you already are might begin "I am Christ, whole and perfect ..."

For one full day, respond to every situation by being the best Christ you can be! Capture your experiences and feelings about this activity in your journal.

> Your responses will vary depending on your own experience. One example: I am driving down the highway and get cut off by another driver. Instead of reacting from personality, yelling and honking my horn, I instead respond from love, feeling grateful they had the space to move in front of me.

Chapter Sixteen—
The Threefold Nature of Humankind—Spirit, Soul and Body

The Heart of the Matter

Summarize this chapter in five sentences or less. Your response may include some of the following concepts:

- The threefold nature of humankind helps us understand the creative process that begins with Spirit and ends in form.
- It helps us understand the relationship between Spirit, soul and body—our Spiritual, mental and physical natures.
- Spirit is what we really are.
- "s" soul is the sum total of our consciousness and subconscious minds.
- Body is "the outer expression of consciousness; the precipitation of the thinking part of man."
- Balancing Spirit, soul and body cultivates wholeness.

Putting It Into Practice

During your daily morning meditation, purposely reflect on the following three questions:

- *What am I going to do today to take care of my body?*
- *What am I going to do today to take care of my soul (mind)?*
- *What am I going to do today to remember I am Spirit?*

Take action on the Divine Ideas that come. Capture the impact of your choices in your journal.

Your responses will vary depending on your own experience, but here are a few examples for each category:

Body Eat right—only have one small desert today; eat three balanced meals; eat so I only consume enough calories to maintain my current weight; lose weight.
Exercise—take a 30 minute walk; go for a run; use the elliptical machine for at least 20 minutes; go to yoga class; lift weights; stretch.

Mind Read the Bible or other inspirational resources.
Pray.
Use denials and affirmations.

Spirit Practice the Silence—a meditation practice that allows you to slip into the Silence.
Meditate using the Centering Prayer.

Chapter Seventeen—The Three Phases of Mind

The Heart of the Matter

Summarize this chapter in five sentences or less. Your response may include some of the following concepts:

- Consciousness is a sense of awareness and knowing.
- The evolution of individual consciousness affects collective consciousness.
- Our minds have consciousness in the One Mind.
- Conscious mind is the phase of our mind from which we function rationally and are aware of our mental processes.
- The subconscious mind stores memories, past thoughts and feelings.
- Superconscious Mind is the I AM, the Christ, God-Mind.
- The Superconscious Mind infuses the subconscious mind with Divine Ideas, clearing and transforming its consciousness.

Putting It Into Practice

Create your own personal guided meditation that takes you on a journey through three levels. (Examples might be a cave experience, diving into a pond or river, or climbing a mountain.) Once you have written this meditation, present it to a small group and then ask for their feedback in terms of how they experienced it.

Your responses will vary depending on your own experience. We are confident by now that you have created a deeply moving meditation that had a powerful impact on the group.

Chapter Eighteen—Personality/Individuality

The Heart of the Matter

Summarize this chapter in five sentences or less. Your response may include some of the following concepts:

- Individuality and personality are two "attitudes" of mind.
- Personality is the sum total of the characteristics and opinions that comprise our current beliefs and concepts about ourselves.
- Personality is always changing.
- The personality is made up of supportive aspects and adverse aspects. These are also called the supportive and adverse egos.
- Individuality is our Real Spiritual Self.
- Individuality is also thought of as how we each uniquely express Christ Consciousness.
- Self-observation allows us to know if we are living from personality (ego) or Individuality.

Putting It Into Practice

Gather lots of creative tools, such as markers, paint, ribbon, yarn, paste, paper plates, brown paper bags. Using these tools, create a mask that reflects something about your personality.

Enjoy this creative activity, designing a mask that clearly reflects something about you that makes up your earthly persona.

Put your mask on or over some kind of light and reflect on how the mask affects the light. Now respond to the following question: Imagine the light reflects your Higher Self, while the mask you created represents your personality/ego, which is the "bushel basket" you hold over your light that keeps it from shining as brightly as it can. What does your bushel basket look like—and what can you do to let your light shine?

Your responses will vary depending on your own experience. Notice the effect of the mask and the light, which will vary depending on the material of your mask. If your mask is opaque, there will be little or no light shining through. This could represent a time when you are strongly in your personality/ego. On the other hand, with a translucent mask, a lot of light will shine through, representing a time when little ego is in play and you are operating from your highest Christ self.

In terms of how you can let your light shine brighter, a few ideas are: Simply be aware of how strong your ego can be and choose not to react from it; create a regular spiritual practice of prayer and meditation; choose to take a deep breath as you experience what you perceive to be an adverse situation. (The pause created by this deep breath provides a doorway to allowing your Christ nature to shine.)

Chapter Nineteen—The Four Functions of Consciousness

The Heart of the Matter

Summarize this chapter in five sentences or less. Your response may include some of the following concepts:

- The four functions of consciousness are thinking, feeling, sensing and intuiting.
- Sensing refers to our use of the five senses to experience the outer world.
- Thinking is the formulating process of mind known as the intellect, which translates what we sense as well as Divine Inspiration from our Divine Nature into mental concepts.
- Feeling is the function of consciousness by which thoughts are empowered and made personal.
- Intuiting is direct inner knowing. It is the function by which we become aware of Divine Ideas.
- We must balance our use of the four functions of consciousness.

Putting It Into Practice

Over the course of several days, simply observe how you interact with the world around you. Discern which of the four functions you use the most. You might even rank them from the most to the least used. Once you are aware of the function(s) you primarily use, you can then begin to consciously practice using the others. Your goal is to use all four in the most balanced way possible.

Your responses will vary depending on your own experience, but here are some examples to help you.

An example of using your sensing function: You are looking for a new home. Upon entering one house, the first thing you notice is the smell of freshly baked cookies. You become aware that you love other things about the home because of this first positive sensation.

An example of using your thinking function: As you go about your normal day, you realize you tend to analyze and ruminate on everything.

An example of using your feeling function: In your annual review, you notice you are reacting emotionally to what your supervisor says, before you think about whether it is valid or not.

An example of using your intuiting function: As you interview candidates for a position, you automatically know who will be the best person for the job even though the résumé may not reflect this.

The next time you notice your feeling nature is strongly engaged, try this:
A. *Feeling: Simply allow yourself to be aware of the feelings, noticing how you are experiencing these feelings.*
B. *Sensing: Be aware of what information you are gleaning from your senses. What are you hearing, seeing, smelling, touching, tasting?*

C. *Thinking: Rationally look at the information you are getting from your senses and reflect on times you had a similar reaction. What are you believing now that is the impetus for what you are feeling?*

D. *Intuiting: Get still, breathe and center yourself. If you have time, meditate for a while and notice if any new ideas or thoughts pop into your awareness. How are you going to use these ideas to change your experience?*

Your responses will vary depending on your own experience. Here's an example: Imagine you are out walking and you see a good friend across the street. You wave to her, but she does not respond and just keeps on walking.

a. Feeling: You experience immediate feelings of hurt and sadness at being rejected and ignored.

b. Sensing: You did not see or hear any response from your friend.

c. Thinking: As you reflect on this experience, you begin to recall multiple times when you felt rejected and ignored by other people. You begin to notice you have a strong belief that people do not really love you and will eventually reject and ignore you. You also realize that it could be as simple as that person not even seeing you.

d. Intuiting: During your meditation time, you become more in touch with your true Christ nature, as well as affirm the Christ nature in the other person.

As a way to heighten your awareness of the four functions of consciousness, practice the art of "The Four Questions." Throughout your day, periodically stop in the midst of whatever situation you're involved in, pause, and ask yourself these four questions:

A. What am I thinking?

B. What am I feeling?

C. What am I sensing?

D. What am I intuiting?

The order in which you ask them is not important; just be sure you explore all four questions. Next reflect on what you are experiencing in a deliberate, balanced way. You might notice you need to more consciously increase your use of one function or another.

Your responses will vary depending on your own experience. Here's an example:

You are cooking dinner and you ask yourself the four questions. Your responses may be something like this:

• What am I feeling? I notice I have a sense of joy and happiness.

• What am I sensing? I am sensing the smell and texture of the food I am cooking. I taste some of the ingredients as I prepare the food. I hear the food sizzling in the frying pan.

- What am I intuiting? At first, I am not intuiting anything! From a purely human perspective, after a quick taste of the food, I intuit what seasonings need to be added. At a higher level, my joy and happiness expand my awareness to realize the true Christ nature of each of my friends who will be sharing in this party.

Chapter Twenty—Thought/Feeling

The Heart of the Matter

Summarize the chapter in five sentences or less. Your response may include some of the following concepts:

- Each person has dominion over thoughts, emotions, feelings and passions.
- All cause is in the realm of mind/Mind.
- Effects are the result of thoughts held in mind.
- The power of thought shapes and forms consciousness and our world.
- When we use the term *thought* in Unity, we almost always mean the combined energies of thought and feeling.
- The Law of Mind action states that thoughts held in mind produce after their kind.
- Like individual consciousness, the collective consciousness contains a mixture of true and error beliefs.
- Consciousness is usually changed "one thought/feeling at a time."

Putting It Into Practice

Become aware of a situation where you notice you are having undesirable, uncomfortable thoughts (for example, you planned a golf game and it is raining. You are thinking, "What a bummer! Why does it have to rain the one day I want to play golf?"). As soon as you become aware of your thoughts, identify what feelings are going along with those thoughts. Consciously change the thought. How does that affect your feelings?

Your responses will vary depending on your own experience. In the example of the rained-out golf game, you consciously change your thought to "Wow! I now have four hours I can fill up in any way I want! What a great gift of time!" This affects your feelings because you notice you are already feeling lighter and happier about the situation.

Become aware of a situation in which you realize you are feeling uncomfortable (for example, you are in a meeting and your idea was shot down by others. You realize your fists are clenched, your stomach is queasy, and you are feeling a warm flush to your face.) As soon as you become aware of your feelings, identify what thoughts are accompanying them. Consciously change the feeling (take a couple of slow, deep breaths, relax your hands, roll your shoulders) and notice how the change affects your thoughts.

Your responses will vary depending on your own experience. In the example above, as you take the deep breaths, relax your hands, and roll your shoulders, you become aware that you can respond differently. You begin to listen to the feedback from others and realize your idea could be adapted in a better way to be more effective.

Chapter Twenty-One—The Word

The Heart of the Matter

Summarize this chapter in five sentences or less Your response may include some of the following concepts:

- Logos is the creative Principle in action.
- Logos = the Word = Christ.
- Words, especially those infused with feeling, carry incredible power.
- Words get their originating power from Divine Ideas.
- Divine Ideas are modified by collective consciousness and then are further modified by individual consciousness.
- The most powerful of all spoken words are words of Truth.
- Singing is one use of the power of the word that can change gloomy thinking and bring harmony to the body.
- Formative words are primarily informed and empowered from personality.
- Creative words are primarily informed and empowered from Individuality.

Putting It Into Practice

Employ the Backward Glance Technique, using the following chart to help you.

Your responses will vary depending on your own experience. Here is an example of how you could use the chart. Imagine it was completed moving from the far right side backward to the far left, ending with The Christ.

Example: Writing my first book!

The Christ (The Word)	Divine Ideas	Thoughts/Feelings	Words you associate with this activity/event
The Christ	Wisdom; Imagination; Order	Excitement; a little fear (can I do it?); opportunity	Creative; educational; sharing knowledge; new; exciting

When you find yourself in a conversation about the economy and realize it is spiraling negatively, find a way to shift the consciousness of the conversation. Become aware of your own thoughts and feelings as you focus on different words to interject into the conversation.

Realize that the issue of the economy is derived from the Divine Idea of Prosperity/Abundance. Think of words that reflect the Divine Idea of Abundance and use them to shift the conversation from the "optical delusion" of lack. For example, you might say something like: "One positive experience I've had with increased gas prices is becoming more aware of how to plan my trips, and I find I have more time in the long run, and my money seems to be doing more for me than ever before!"

Chapter Twenty-Two—Denials and Affirmations

The Heart of the Matter

Summarize this chapter in five sentences or less. Your response may include some of the following concepts:

- Denials and affirmations are tools for cleansing consciousness—"the conscious and subconscious minds."
- The use of denials and affirmations engages both the thinking and feeling natures.
- Denials release the energy and power we have given error thoughts, feelings and beliefs.
- Denials are in the first person, present tense.
- Denials are generally spoken gently with conviction.
- Affirmations confirm and claim Divine Ideas.
- Affirmations are formulated and spoken after Truth is realized.
- Affirmations are first person, present tense, positive and spoken with Power.
- Affirmations raise consciousness and facilitate bringing Divine Ideas from the unformed to the formed.

Putting It Into Practice

Make a list of your most frustrating emotions/fears. Create five denials and five replacement affirmations of Truth. Repeat these several times throughout the day, every day for 30 days. Become aware of the difference this makes in how you think and feel.

Your responses will vary depending on your own experience. Here's an example:

The frustrating emotion/fear might be fear of rejection. A denial: "I give no power to the seeming fear of rejection." An affirmation: *I am Christ. I am love. I am lovable.*

Another example could be a fear of heights. A denial: "I dissolve the fear I have when I am in high places." An affirmation: *My Consciousness is greater than any feeling of fear of heights I experience.*

Employ what we call the "Fillmore Challenge." The following statement is attributed to both Charles and Myrtle, depending on the source, but essentially what they said was this: "Never make an assertion, no matter how true it may look on the surface, that you do not want to see manifest in your life!" This is so powerful! Something as simple as the statement "I'm having a bad hair day" is something you do not want to see manifest—so why would you give power to it through your words? Set a goal of moving through an entire day without saying anything you do not want to see manifest in your life. This is an incredibly inspiring adventure—and one that will serve you well!

We encourage you to track your experience as you attempt to move through an entire day using the Fillmore Challenge. You might even want to chart how many days it takes before you actually go an entire day without asserting anything you do not want to see manifest in your life.

Chapter Twenty-Three—Creation

The Heart of the Matter

Summarize this chapter in five sentences or less. Your response may include some of the following concepts:

- The starting point is always Oneness, Source.
- Creation is the process by which formless Divine Ideas become manifest form.
- Mind-idea-expression (one definition of Divine Order) is one way to define the creative process.
- Humankind creates from Divine Ideas.
- Humankind limits, molds and shapes Divine Ideas. Your responses will vary depending on your own experience.
- What Divine Mind created (ideated) is finished.

Putting It Into Practice

Look around your home or office. Choose five items that are particularly meaningful to you. For each item, identify the Divine Idea underwriting it and reflect on three other ways that Divine Idea could have manifested.

I have a beautiful scented candle with a prosperity affirmation about money wrapped around it. One Divine Idea underwriting it is Beauty. Other ways these Divine Ideas could be expressed are: A landscaped garden, a painting, a dance choreographed to a Chopin nocturne, a song by Secret Garden.

Think of your favorite hobby or passion. How do you use mind-idea-expression to experience that hobby/passion and create activities associated with it?

Your responses will vary depending on your own experience. For example, suppose you have a passion for ballroom dancing. The idea that arises in mind is a desire to compete with your partner in a major competition at the amateur level. In order to bring that idea into expression, you realize you will need to send in your application, make the necessary hotel reservations, create the appropriate dance routines with your coach, and then put in practice time with your dance partner in order to be ready.

Chapter Twenty-Four—The Twelve Powers and

Chapter Twenty-Five—Developing the Twelve Powers

The Heart of the Matter (Chapter 24)

Summarize this chapter in five sentences or less. Your response may include some of the following concepts:

- The Twelve Powers are the 12 fundamental aspects of our Divine Nature.
- The Twelve Powers exist in our minds as 12 Divine Ideas.
- Each disciple metaphysically represents a corresponding Power.
- A color is associated with each Power.
- A location is associated with each Power.
- The Twelve Powers are Faith, Strength, Wisdom, Love, Power, Imagination, Understanding, Will, Order, Zeal, Elimination, Life.

The Heart of the Matter (Chapter 25)

Summarize this chapter in five sentences or less. Your response may include some of the following concepts:

- Our goal is to express the Christ Potential as fully as possible.
- Degeneration is a collective and individual fall in consciousness.
- Generation is procreation.
- Regeneration is the process of quickening and "repurposing" each of the Twelve Powers. It regenerates the Christ Ideas.
- Avoid the temptation to use the Powers for personal gain.
- Developing the Twelve Powers involves the awareness of them as well as investing time in meditation.
- Denials and affirmations can be used to develop the Twelve Powers.

Putting It Into Practice (Chapters 24 and 25)

Focus on a Power a day during your meditation time. See how many ways you can bring that focus to your meditation.

> The way in which you accomplish this will vary, but here is one example: Suppose you decided to focus on the Power of Imagination. During your meditation time you visualize the color of Imagination (sky blue) around the area of the third eye. You might imagine the "white light" of Christ energizing the area of the third eye. Then you imagine and visualize yourself going about the day using this Power of Imagination. You open yourself up to becoming aware of thoughts and feelings stimulated by Divine Ideas. Then you create visual images of how you could put those thoughts and feelings into action. Of course, you then must take the action necessary to manifest those thoughts and feelings.

Choose to use a "Power of the day" as you go about your regular activities. Keep that Power in your conscious awareness, checking out how you are using it throughout your day, as well as investing time in retrospect at the end of your day, critiquing your effectiveness with using the Power at your highest, most elevated level.

The way in which you accomplish this will vary, but here is one example: You have chosen the Power of Imagination to focus on for the day. During the day, when you stop to assess how you are doing, you notice you are mentally tired and have been worrying about possible layoffs in your company. You realize you have been using your Power of Imagination at a lower level of effectiveness to imagine what your life would be like after being fired. At this point you can choose to call upon a more elevated level of Imagination to visualize something different, something more supportive. Throughout the day, you remind yourself of the Power of Imagination by posting reminder notes, connecting with things that are light blue, and setting a timer to go off periodically to trigger yourself to focus on the Power of the day.

At the end of the day, you reflect on how you made the conscious choice to change the way in which you were using the Power of Imagination and notice the positive impact it had on your energy level and your attitude, as well as your productivity.

After a meeting or social event, use the Power of Judgment to assess how it went. Ask yourself questions such as:

a. *Did I actively engage the Powers as I had intended prior to the event?*

b. *What other Powers could I have engaged once the event was in progress?*

c. *Was I informing the Powers primarily from my ego/personality?*

d. *Was I at least attempting to inform their use from a higher level of consciousness?*

The way in which you accomplish this will vary, and here is one example: The day after you attended a family gathering for Thanksgiving dinner, you decide to evaluate how the celebration went. You turn to the questions and answer one by one.

A. *Did I actively engage the Powers as I had intended prior to the event?*

Yes, I did pretty well using the Power of Judgment to monitor how much wine I drank. I even used the Power of Dominion in controlling my ego to avoid getting into an argument over some minor political discussion. I did pretty well.

B. *What other Powers could I have engaged once the event was in progress?*

I sure could have engaged the Power of Strength better. I had intended to not overeat this year. But when Grandma offered me a second piece of pumpkin pie, I crumbled. I had it with a good spritz of whipped cream too! I very quickly went from being a bit over-full to being overstuffed—like the turkey! I could have deliberately engaged the Power of Strength to stay the course with my intention to not overeat this year, even in the face of Grandma's loving insistence.

C. *Was I informing the Powers primarily from my ego/personality?*

Well, when I was tempted to become argumentative, I sure noticed how I started to engage my Powers from my ego. However, as soon as I noticed, I stopped myself. Hmmm ... this means I engaged the Power of Dominion to control myself. I also engaged the Power of Elimination by saying "No" to my instinct to attack arising from my ego/personality.

D. *Was I at least attempting to inform their use from a higher level of consciousness?*

Hey, I did pretty well. Just when I was about to react from my personality I stopped myself. Then I responded from a higher level of awareness. I was kind and loving. Last year I might have been extremely argumentative. This means I truly engaged my Powers of Love, Dominion, Elimination, Understanding, Judgment and Will to choose the higher road.

Each day you can actively decide to practice a Power, use a Power, from a more supportive ego/personality level and especially from as high a level of consciousness as possible. Consciously use the Powers to be the best person or the best Christ you can be!

The way in which you respond to this will vary depending on your experience, but here is one illustration:

From the Personality: During your observations, you notice your Powers of Elimination and Order are both underdeveloped. This is evidenced by the disorder in the accumulation of stuff in your garage, basement and desk. You decide to begin by working with the Power of Elimination. To be sure, you also know Judgment and Understanding will be engaged, and yet, your focus for this activity is on Elimination. For just this one day, you decide to use the Power of Elimination to get rid of the stuff you no longer need or that is no longer serving you. You find ways to repurpose or give away the stuff that still has usefulness; other stuff, you simply throw away.

From the Higher Consciousness: During your day, you decide to use the Power of Elimination to be the best person, even the Christ you already are. Calling on the Power of Elimination, you say "No" to any urge to act from lower states of consciousness. For example, you use it to eliminate any negative judgments you are having about the people with whom you work.

At the end of your day, reflect on what Powers you have used and from what level of consciousness. Can you identify how you have used all Twelve Powers? If so, which ones and when? The intent is to become very conscious of the Powers so that you more actively use them every day.

The way in which you respond to this will vary depending on your experience, but here is one example:

• *At the end of your day, reflect on what Powers you have used and from what level of consciousness.* As I come to the end of my day and invest the time to reflect on how I used the Twelve Powers, I recall several exchanges I had throughout the day. One I recall vividly is a meeting with a colleague, Alice. I realize that negative judgments of Alice began to arise immediately during my meeting with her. At first, I used the Power of Elimination from a low state of consciousness to deny any loving and kind thoughts arising to counter the negative judgments. Then, very consciously, I decided to use that Power from a higher, more elevated consciousness by denying any power or credence to the negative judgments of Alice. This decision brought my focus onto more kind and loving thoughts, and I began to see Alice through my "Christ eyes."

- *Can you identify whether you have used all Twelve Powers? If so, which ones and when?* I used several other Powers today:

    1. Faith – I believe in Christ, the True Nature of each and every person and therefore in Alice.
    2. Strength – I stayed the course in being the Christ I already am. I demonstrated this when I chose to see Alice from my Christ eyes instead of from my ego.
    3. Judgment – I discerned the Christ when I interacted with Alice.
    4. Love – I desired to see Alice's Christ Nature and not my ego judgments of her.
    5. Dominion – I controlled my ego nature while I began to master my ability to be the Christ I already am.
    6. Imagination – From the start of the day, I visualized myself being Christ in each and every situation. I also visualized myself being Christ, living from Divine Ideas such as the Twelve Powers that I am working with today.
    7. Understanding – I know what makes up Christ Consciousness (for example, Prosperity, Oneness, the Twelve Powers) as well as know about my ego, personality (for example, separation, anger, fear).
    8. Will – I chose to be more Christ than personality.
    9. Order – I am aware I went about this in an orderly way. I also noticed how I used mind-idea-expression.
    10. Zeal – This Power was not so evident, though at the beginning of the day I was fairly enthusiastic about how well I might do.
    11. Elimination – Explored above.
    12. Life – I certainly vitalized and enlivened my day when I chose my Higher Nature over my ego.

Note: You can explore the Twelve Powers in much more detail by taking the Spiritual Education and Enrichment class The Twelve Powers and by reading the book *PowerUP: The Twelve Powers Revisited as Accelerated Abilities*, by Paul Hasselbeck and Cher Holton.

Chapter Twenty-Six—The Kingdom of Heaven—The Fourth Dimension

The Heart of the Matter

Summarize this chapter in five sentences or less. Your response may include some of the following concepts:

- The essence of Oneness blends and harmonizes all things.
- The Kingdom of God is the Absolute, the Infinite "Field" of Potential and Possibilities.
- The Kingdom of Heaven is the realm of Divine Ideas.
- The Kingdom of Heaven is also referred to as the Fourth Dimension and the Garden of Eden.
- There are seven Dimensions. Dimensions four through seven do not correspond to dimensions that have been discovered by science.
- The Seventh Dimension is Universal Mass, the Absolute, the field of infinite potential and possibilities.
- The Sixth Dimension is motion.
- The Fifth Dimension is where the "elements/Divine Ideas" begin to separate out.
- The Fourth Dimension is the realm of Divine Ideas; the assembly and disassembly point of Divine Ideas.
- Dimensions one through three are of the physical realm.
- Everything that is seen comes out of the unseen.
- Everything is either progressing from or resolving back into the Universal Mass.

Putting It Into Practice

We call this technique "reverse engineering." Go visit a favorite landscaped area (such as a park, garden, your own backyard). Just devote time observing the area. Now, step by step, work backward by identifying how this area was created.

> Your responses will vary depending on what site you visited. Here is an abbreviated example of what you might record:
>
> I am looking at a beautiful landscaped yard. The flowers grew and blossomed. Weeds were removed. Plantings and seeds were planted. The ground was prepared. Plantings and seeds were purchased. The hardscape was completed. Rocks and cement were purchased. A plan was drawn up, taking into consideration the lighting, lay of the land, and other factors affecting the landscape decisions. The landscaper saw the property and walked over it, taking into account what would be best in this location. The landscaper had an idea of what this yard could potentially look like. The beginning was the Divine Idea of Beauty.

There are several Divine Ideas that underwrite the landscaped area you are viewing. Identify some of them and how each Idea is manifested in the landscape.

> Again, your responses will vary, but examples would be:

Beauty: Manifested as the flowers, trees, sculptures, visual impact of how all the elements come together;

Order: Manifested in the way in which things were done to effectively create the landscape.

Will: Manifested as the choices made by the landscaper based on understanding how the various plants would be affected by the lighting, soil and terrain.

Chapter Twenty-Seven—The Creative Process

The Heart of the Matter

Summarize this chapter in five sentences or less. Your response may include some of the following concepts:

- God creates/ideates Divine Ideas through mind action.
- The Spiritual Universe is made up of Divine Ideas.
- Everything in the material universe is based upon Divine Ideas.
- Through meditation and prayer, Substance is quickened and appropriated.
- God created/ideated the Spiritual Universe.
- Chaos or the void precedes the first step.
- First day/first step: Light is Illumination and Understanding.
- Second day/second step: Faith is belief in Divine Ideas and believing in the Divine Laws that make manifestation possible. It is the separation of Divine Ideas from the Infinite Field.
- Third day/third step: Imagination is used to give more and more shape and form in consciousness.
- Fourth day/fourth step: Understanding and Will are used to know what is needed and Will chooses what is needed.
- Fifth Day/fifth step: Discrimination is used to compare what we know.
- Sixth Day/sixth step: Love and Wisdom are used to wisely desire what we want.
- Seventh Day/seventh step: Sabbath is when we rest in the realization that our good is coming.

Putting It Into Practice

Choose something you have created. (This can be anything you have made, ranging from a recipe you created to artwork, poetry or journal entries, a dance choreography, a Play-Doh sculpture.) Take each of the steps of the Creative Process and identify how you employed them in your creation.

Your response will vary depending on what specific creation you select. The key to this activity is to work backward so you get a visual image of how everything begins with a Divine Idea, and how each step along the way refines the Idea, bringing it into manifestation based on choices you make. Here is one example, to get you started.

Let's say you've created a new website. Let's explore how you used the seven steps of the creative process to create it in consciousness first.

- First day/first step: This is where you get a glimmer of the idea to reach out to other people.
- Second day/second step: Here, you begin to believe it is possible to have a really jazzy website as your way of reaching out to people. You become aware of all the different ideas and elements you might include.
- Third day/third step: In this phase, you use your Power of Imagination to give the website idea more form and shape in consciousness.

- Fourth day/fourth step: Now you begin to collect what you know about what you want on your website, and you use Will to make particular choices about layout, design and content.

- Fifth Day/fifth step: During this phase, you begin to compare and contrast all the elements and sections you have developed in consciousness, to determine priorities and locations for each section of the website.

- Sixth Day/sixth step: Now that we have the website designed in consciousness, we use our Powers of Love and Wisdom to bring it into manifestation. We desire a powerful and meaningful website with a design and content that people are attracted to.

- Seventh Day/seventh step: At this point, we rest in the knowing that the perfect website will be manifested.

Think of an idea you have that you would like to bring into manifestation. Using the steps of the Creative Process, write a plan of action to move the idea into actualization.

Again, your plan of action will be specific and unique to you. Be aware of how you are using the Creative Process to bring a sense of control to your ability to manifest ideas. This process will be very similar to what we just described in the activity above.

Twenty-Eight—Stumbling Blocks and Keys to Demonstration

The Heart of the Matter

Summarize this chapter in five sentences or less. Your response may include some of the following concepts:

- Demonstration is always occurring whether we like the results or not.
- Stumbling blocks and obstacles are primarily in the mind as thoughts and feelings.
- Zeal's quiet passion coupled with Dominion's power to master and control helps to bring all thoughts and feelings into line to demonstrate good.
- Focusing on the negative or dwelling in fear increases the negativity and fear in consciousness and can result in outpicturing them in the physical realm.
- Joy dissolves the blocks to demonstration (uneasiness, fears, doubts and discouraged states of mind).
- Attachment to the outer realm hinders awareness of the Oneness and Substance inhibiting demonstration.
- Nonattachment smoothes the path to demonstration.
- Resisting, fighting and opposing unwanted thoughts hinder demonstration by increasing them in consciousness.
- Nonresistance eliminates an oppositional attitude.
- Nonresistance does not necessarily equate to nonaction.
- Forgiveness and repentance clear the blocks to demonstration by moving awareness from the outer realm to the inner realm of Truth and Oneness.
- It becomes easier and easier to consciously demonstrate as consciousness rises.
- All demonstration begins from the awareness of Divine Mind, or Oneness.
- Divine Mind is the source of Divine Ideas.
- Everything in the physical or manifest realms has its basis in Divine Ideas, which are the beginning point of all demonstration.
- Practicing the Silence through meditation results in Divine Ideas arising into awareness as related thoughts, feelings, illumination, guidance and elevated viewpoints.
- Prayer focuses attention and intention on what is desired.
- Prayer results in the realization of Divine Ideas, which are then claimed and from which good is manifested.
- Concentration focuses attention and intention on the ideas and thoughts of what is desired, gathering the thought forces used in manifestation. The outer resources are then perceived for manifesting what is desired.
- Realization is a deep inner conviction, knowing what is desired will be demonstrated despite outer appearances.
- Substance is our Supply. Substance is Divine Ideas.
- Substance is molded in consciousness to manifest what is desired.
- All Twelve Powers are used to manifest and demonstrate.

- Faith linked with Imagination is the impetus for moving Divine Ideas from the unseen to the seen.

- Love (the ability to desire) must be used in conjunction with Understanding (the ability to know and understand) and Wisdom (the ability to apply what is known) so that good for everyone is demonstrated.

- Love that is *not* tempered by Understanding and Wisdom results in erroneous demonstrations and undesirable outcomes.

- Love and Order harmonize and balance all aspects of demonstration.

- Peace and harmony create a receptive condition of mind, ensuring demonstration.

- Thoughts and feelings create the mental atmosphere from which a person perceives the world.

- Use thoughts and feelings to focus on what is desired so you are able to recognize what is needed in the outer world for demonstration.

- The spoken word closely aligned with Divine Ideas has the power to manifest desires according to the level of consciousness of the speaker.

- Denials brush away and disempower any identified obstacles to demonstration.

- Affirmations claim what is already True in Consciousness.

- Praise, bless and be grateful for the Oneness we are in Truth.

- Praise, bless and be grateful for what you want to demonstrate.

- Pair up visualization (Power of Imagination) with the Power of the Word, affirming and talking only about good.

- Patience based on Faith, Understanding and Strength is needed if demonstration does not come quickly.

Putting It Into Practice

For each of the following situations, identify what you believe to be the primary stumbling block: fear, attachment, resistance or unforgiveness. For each situation, create a plan of action to overcome the stumbling block and move toward manifestation. We will be calling each plan of action a "prescription" and use the medical symbol "Rx" to represent it.

> a. *You have made the decision to deepen your spiritual practice by using a daily time for meditation using Centering Prayer. As you begin doing this, you find your "monkey mind thoughts" are interfering. The more you try to control and quiet them, the louder and more annoying they become. You are ready to conclude that Centering Prayer is not a technique that works for you.*

STUMBLING BLOCK: Resistance

Rx: *[Note: Your specific responses will vary, but here is one example of what the Rx could look like.]* Recall the section from *Heart-Centered Metaphysics* covering Resistance/Nonresistance, and recognize that "Monkey Mind type chatter" is actually part of your meditation practice. Rather than fight or resist it, you choose to stay nonresistant. You acknowledge the chatter ("Thank you for sharing") then use your mantra to return to center. (You can read more on Centering Prayer in Chapter 7 of *Heart-Centered Metaphysics.*)

b. *You want to apply for a job that would be a great step up for you, both financially and professionally. As you begin to complete the application, you realize your qualifications aren't strong enough and believe you could never be selected. You panic at the thought of the interview, which includes a presentation to an interview team. You are ready to tear up the application and remain in the comfortable, safe, unfulfilling job you now have.*

STUMBLING BLOCK: Fear

Rx: *[Note: Your specific responses will vary, but here is one example of what the Rx could look like.]* Face the fear. Acknowledge the real obstacles are your inner fears: fear of failure; fear of rejection; fear of public speaking; even fear of success. Once you name your fears, create denials to withdraw any power you have given them, and follow up with dynamic, Truth-centered affirmations. [See Chapter 22 in *Heart-Centered Metaphysics* for more information on Denials and Affirmations.] Use visualization to see yourself rising to your highest level of consciousness and potential to claim this new position. Identify any real gaps you have and take steps to address them (for example, work with a speech coach to enhance your public speaking skill).

c. *A few years ago, you were devastated when your partner ended your relationship. You still harbor feelings of anger, hurt and resentment, and continue to replay the incident in your mind, formulating all kinds of judgments about your former partner and the way in which the break-up happened. You share your "sad story" whenever you can, relishing the negative feelings and scenarios you can relate. The blame is all on your former partner and what was done "to" you. As you begin a new relationship with someone different, you find yourself bringing up all the old stories, feeling the pain all over again.*

STUMBLING BLOCK: Unforgiveness

Rx: *[Note: Your specific responses will vary, but here is one example of what the Rx could look like.]* Remember the real issue is not what someone else did "to you," but how you perceive and deal with it. Even though the relationship ended years ago, it is still fresh because you are continuing to feed it in your consciousness. It is time to practice forgiveness. You may want to create a symbolic act of this, such as a burning bowl experience, a burial or a guided meditation. Invoke the Divine Powers of Release and Love, and allow them to infuse your being. Affirm your Oneness, and visualize harmony and peace for yourself and your former partner. Note the wonderful, positive things you remember about the relationship, then use appreciation and gratitude to raise your feeling nature to its most elevated level and allow your creative power of thought to manifest your right and perfect relationship.

d. *You have found the "perfect house" you want to purchase. You know this is the house for you! You find yourself feeling nervous and worried about getting your current house sold, and having your offer for the "perfect house" accepted, so you will be able to buy that "per-*

fect house."

STUMBLING BLOCK: Attachment

Rx: *[Note: Your specific responses will vary, but here is one example of what the Rx could look like.]* As you become aware of your strong attachment to this specific house, go into the Silence and be still. Affirm Oneness and affirm the Truth of Abundance and Divine Substance. Call forth the Divine Ideas of Release, Order and Dominion. Focus on visualizing the essence of what you desire, knowing the potential channels for manifestation are limitless. Be open, receptive and aware of specific, actionable thoughts and feelings that will provide a solution.

Chapter Twenty-Nine Metaphysical Basis for Wholeness and Health

The Heart of the Matter

Summarize this chapter in five sentences. Your response may include some of the following concepts:

- Divine Mind ideates (creates) the perfect pattern or the "perfect Body Idea," which is the fundamental basis of the pure potential for health and wholeness inherent in humankind.
- Staying centered in the awareness of Divine Mind as perfect Life in Consciousness facilitates the expression of the fullness of our Beingness.
- The body is manifested from the Divine Idea of Body (the perfect Body Idea) by and from collective and individual consciousness.
- Life, wholeness and health manifest according to the activity of the Law of Mind Action and Divine Order (Mind/mind–Idea/idea–Expression/expression).
- Identify with the Divine Idea of Life within consciousness in order to experience an ever-increasing awareness of wholeness, health and vitality—first in mind, then in body.
- Life reveals health and wholeness.
- Our thoughts direct how the energy within our cells function and is sustained. This intelligence directs how Life acts upon Substance.
- Love lacks volition and does not discriminate. Therefore, it works best in conjunction with Wisdom, Understanding and Will.
- Keeping our thoughts centered on the Divine Idea of Life facilitates the realization of Wholeness.
- The Principle of Health underlies and pervades everything.

Putting It Into Practice

Journal about your personal beliefs related to the condition of your physical body. Now reflect on what the perfect Body Idea might be in Divine Mind. Compare and contrast the two and notice any stumbling blocks to attaining the body you desire.

> While your responses will vary based on your personal reflections, an example would be: You believe you are out of shape, and at the same time, you know that the perfect Body Idea of wholeness and health would normally express as a body that is in shape. You note that one of your stumbling blocks is a belief and fear that you cannot achieve the goal of a body in good shape. So you use denials to disempower the belief and fear, you begin visualizing yourself in shape, and you create an affirmation to support this.

Design a poster that captures the essence of your "Perfect Body Idea Credo." This poster can include visuals that reflect and inspire you, as well as denials and affirmative statements that capture the Truth of the Perfect Body Idea manifesting as you. Use the Perfect Body Idea Credo as a daily reminder of the power you have to manifest your wholeness and health.

Your Perfect Body Idea Credo and poster will be unique to you. One way you might achieve this is to find a picture of a similar body type to you that is in good physical shape. Then paste a current picture of your head on that body. Other elements of your poster might include pictures of a person working out, an ice cream soda with the "NO" symbol over it and inspiring words.

Chapter Thirty—Stumbling Blocks and Keys to Demonstrating Life, Wholeness and Health

The Heart of the Matter

Summarizing this chapter in five sentences or less. Your response may include some of the following concepts:

- Demonstration can occur when Life, wholeness and health are realized and claimed in consciousness.
- Stumbling blocks to demonstrating health and wholeness are always in mind (consciousness).
- Examples of stumbling blocks include the lack of Faith in Oneness, having an outer focus, and imagining all sorts of undesirable expressions in the body.
- Use denials to disempower and overcome fear, a negative attitude, belief in sickness, and the use of "disease-affirming words."
- Use affirmations to claim realized Truth—Life, wholeness and health.
- Joy is the antidote to fear and the negative side.
- Awareness of Oneness is hindered by attachment to the body and outer proof.
- Resisting unwanted thoughts and feelings around sickness and disease actually increases and reinforces them in consciousness hindering the demonstration of wholeness and health.
- Nonresistance eliminates the oppositional attitude set up through resistance.
- Unforgiveness blocks healing.
- Forgiveness and repentance (changing the mind) cleanse the consciousness of error thoughts and feelings related to illness and disease.
- An awakened consciousness of Perfection and Wholeness results in manifesting perfection in mind (consciousness) and then in body.
- Life is an inexhaustible Divine Idea in Divine Mind we use to demonstrate wholeness and health, first in mind and then in body.
- Practicing the Silence through meditation quickens the Divine Idea of Life that cleanses and restores wholeness and health.
- Prayer conditions the mind (consciousness) neutralizing beliefs, thoughts and feelings about illness and disease while restoring wholeness and health through the realization of Life.
- The concentration step of the Five-Step Prayer Process gathers the forces of mind and body around the central Divine Idea of Life.
- The realization of the Divine Idea of Life brings the mind (consciousness) and body into alignment with wholeness and health.
- Divine Mind is the unlimited Substance and Supply from which the body is formed.
- All Twelve Powers are used to manifest and demonstrate the Divine Idea of Life leading to wholeness and health.
- The Power of Faith affirms and activates the Divine Idea of Life.
- Imagination works with Faith to shape Substance according to the Divine Idea of Life.
- Love, Understanding and Wisdom work together to demonstrate what is desired: wholeness and health.

- The Powers of Love and Order bring about balance and harmony. Thoughts and feelings are harmonized to manifest wholeness and health using Divine Law and Order (Mind/mind–Idea/idea–Expression/expression).

- Peace creates a receptive state conducive to the demonstration of wholeness and health.

- Thoughts and feelings can either support disease and illness or wholeness and health.

- The power of our words either builds up illness and disease based on error consciousness or health based on Divine Ideas and Christ Consciousness.

- Denials cleanse the mind (consciousness) of erroneous thoughts and feelings of illness and disease.

- Affirmations build up the consciousness of Life expressing as wholeness and health.

- Praise, bless and be grateful for what you want to increase—wholeness and health.

- Praise, bless and be grateful for the body and the health you have.

- Use the Power of Imagination to visualize wholeness and health. See only wholeness and health regardless of appearances.

- If wholeness and health do not come quickly, call on the Power of Strength and be patient.

Putting It Into Practice

Create a scenario that represents how each of the following stumbling blocks might play out in the relative realm, relating to wholeness and health. Then write a prescription that would help a person overcome that particular stumbling block to their wholeness and health.

   a. Fear and the Negative Side

   b. Attachment

   c. Resistance

   d. Unforgiveness

Your responses will vary but could include things such as:

   a. *Fear and the Negative Side:* Fear of creating ugly big muscles if you work out with weights. Rx: When you go to the gym or even see someone who is fit on the street, you notice that they do not have ugly big muscles. You use this information to create denials and affirmations to overcome the fear and affirm a lovely, fit body.

   b. *Attachment:* Attachment to a specific outcome to a health challenge. Let's say you injured your rotator cuff. You are attached to the idea that you want it to heal very quickly so you can continue your exercise program. However, your physical therapist is telling you it will take three months to heal properly. Rx: While claiming wholeness and health for your rotator cuff, you also claim that the cuff will be healed with ease and grace in an orderly fashion and time.

   c. *Resistance:* Resistance in the form of finding excuses why you are not able to make time for exercise. Rx: You make a list of all the excuses you find yourself using to avoid exercising. Every time you are about to empower one of those excuses, you make the choice to exercise anyway.

d. *Unforgiveness:* Every time you see your ex, you relive things you have not yet forgiven, and almost inevitably you experience a migraine. Rx: You realize it is not about your ex; it is about the things you have not yet released. You begin the process of discerning what you have not yet released and clearing any related beliefs.

Chapter Thirty-One—Metaphysical Basis for Prosperity

The Heart of the Matter

Summarize this chapter in five sentences or less. Your response may include some of the following concepts:

- The goal of true prosperity is the realization and unfoldment of our Divine Potential.
- The abundance of Divine Mind is behind all visible form.
- Substance is likened to "Divine Energy." It is the matrix that is the basis for all form.
- Substance makes all form possible. Substance is Divine Ideas.
- How to get Supply is one thing; how to handle supply is another. The two must balance each other.
- The two-step approach to prosperity: 1) the awareness of Divine Ideas and associated formative thought; 2) taking action on those Divine Ideas and thoughts.
- The Law of Increase says we must use the prosperity we have to increase it.
- The Secondary Law of Increase says that our own prosperity consciousness can positively affect another person's prosperity consciousness.
- There seems to be two worlds: the inner Invisible Realm of our Spiritual Nature and the outer visible world of the senses.
- Our conscious mind is pivotal so we seem to live in both realms simultaneously.
- Our attention determines our state of mind at any given moment.
- The inner approach to prosperity is dependent on our inner Spiritual Realm.
- The outer approach to prosperity is dependent on the material or physical realm based on our senses.
- Belief in exclusive possession is an error that can ruin our enjoyment of prosperity.
- Our bounty and unique talents are to be developed and shared generously under the direction of Divine Wisdom and Understanding.
- Be a good steward of what you already have.
- Giving and receiving are two aspects of the prosperity law that must be exercised if we are to release the flow of abundant good in our consciousness.
- Giving freely is the only valid kind of giving—it is an expression of love and generosity.
- Receiving freely and gratefully completes the law creating balance.
- Tithing is giving with the thought of Divine Mind uppermost in consciousness. We share our tithe wherever we receive our spiritual good.
- Money is the visible evidence of a Divine Idea.
- Money itself is not prosperity.
- Money is a symbol representing invisible, ever-present Mind Substance.

Putting It Into Practice

For an entire week, focus on ways you can and do give. This could include giving money, assistance or help, items that are no longer serving you, etc. Keep track in your journal of how this giving impacts you.

> Your responses will vary but should reflect the impact of giving conscious attention to your giving habits. Examples might include carrying groceries into the house for a neighbor; spontaneously giving money to a friend who wants to purchase a certain item; cleaning out your garage and donating unwanted "stuff" to a charitable organization; giving an exceptional waiter an exceptional tip. You might notice that in doing these things, you feel lighter, freer and more joyous. Perhaps you might even notice that people are giving more to you.

During the course of a day, every time you spend money, take a moment to focus on the concept that this money is a symbol that represents invisible, unlimited, ever-present Mind Substance. Notice how this awareness affects your thoughts and attitudes about money and prosperity and keep track of your experiences in your journal. If you don't notice an appreciable effect in just one day, consider using this practice for a number of days and identify when you begin to notice a change in consciousness about money and prosperity.

> Your responses will vary but should reflect the impact of giving conscious attention to the act of recognizing how money is a symbol of unlimited Mind Substance. It is interesting to notice how long it takes to experience a change—and what effect that change has on your daily habits related to money.

For the next month, set the intention that whenever you tithe or give a love offering, you will pause and remember that this is one way you are putting God first in your life. By donating where you receive your spiritual good, you are creating an outer symbol of the inner knowing there is only One Power and One Presence.

> Your responses will vary and should reflect the impact of tithing with conscious awareness and intention. One thing you might notice is that your tithing is coming from a place of joy and abundance, rather than from a place of obligation or fear.

Chapter 32—Stumbling Blocks and Keys to Demonstrating Prosperity

The Heart of the Matter

Summarize this chapter in five sentences or less. Your response may include some of the following concepts:

- Beliefs, thoughts and feelings held in mind can block or hinder increase. Examples include an adverse condition in consciousness, belief in the outer realm and things such as money as the source of prosperity, or an underdeveloped or misused Power of Love.

- Avoid and eliminate the fear of lack and negative attitudes toward money by focusing the mind on Spirit, laughter and song, as well as using denials and affirmations.

- There is a direct relationship between our prosperity and our being joyful when we give.

- Attachment to the outer realm (money and things) and outer results hinders demonstration.

- An attitude of nonattachment smoothes the path to demonstration.

- Resistance to thoughts of lack hinders demonstration by actually increasing those thoughts in consciousness.

- Nonresistance creates a consciousness where we attract ourselves to what is worthwhile, and what is not worthwhile fades away.

- Unforgiveness keeps us from the cleansing power of Spirit and Spiritual Substance.

- Forgiveness and repentance are the exchange of unforgiving thoughts of someone wronging you for the empowering thoughts of love, justice and peace.

- Growth in prosperity consciousness depends more and more on Spirit. Emphasize the Powers of Faith, Wisdom and Understanding so as to balance needs and wants (the Power of Love) while eliminating wastefulness (the Power of Elimination).

- Divine Mind and Divine Ideas are the starting point of all true prosperity. Enliven, awaken and bring into righteous use all the indwelling Resources of Spirit and use them in loving service.

- Divine Ideas are the only true wealth for they are the Primary Causes for all that is good in life.

- Practicing the Silence through meditation puts Divine Mind first and ensures a state of receptivity to the prospering Ideas of Spirit.

- The purpose of affirmative prayer is to express Substance Ideas in material form by connecting Substance Ideas to ideas of material expression.

- Concentrate on Divine Ideas that relate to abundance and prosperity in order to have good results.

- Realization of the Truth of unlimited Resources that are already ours, combined with the elimination of any anxious thoughts of lack and limitation, fulfills the law of prosperity.

- Substance and Supply are Divine Ideas as well as the Universal Matrix in which Divine Ideas of prosperity germinate and grow.

- Each person can control and use Substance constructively, depending entirely on the level of understanding and the proper handling of the Ideas and Substance.

- The awakening and conscious use of the Twelve Powers are important to demonstrating prosperity.

- Faith in Divine Ideas, Laws and Principles in Divine Mind, linked with the Power of Imagination (ability to shape and mold the one Substance), assures abundance.
- The Power of Love is used to desire prosperity and abundance; it works best when combined with the Powers of Wisdom, Understanding and Zeal, resulting in righteous use.
- Through the Powers of Love and Wisdom, we harmonize with divine Law, Ideas and Principles to enjoy a full measure of joy and experience harmony in life.
- A peaceful mind greatly aids the demonstration of prosperity.
- Thoughts, feelings and words govern the demonstration of prosperity.
- Pour living words of Faith into omnipresent Substance and the subconscious mind brings prosperity and abundance into manifestation.
- Use denials to clear and release any negative or error thoughts of fear or lack.
- Use affirmations to build up the Truth of abundance and prosperity.
- Invest time and energy in blessing, praising and expressing gratitude for all that you have.
- Become more conscious of the presence of universal Substance through blessings, praising and gratitude so that It increases for you and the common good of all.
- Using the Power of Imagination, visualize and conceptualize what you desire. See only the Good, the reality of ever-present Substance and Divine Ideas, without regard to outer appearances.
- Patience and trust (the Power of Faith) ease whatever waiting period there may be for the demonstration of prosperity to appear.

Putting It Into Practice:

Quickly, without any judgment or thought, complete the following statement in 10 different ways. Use whatever pops into your mind.

When it comes to the topic of prosperity, I believe . . .

1. _____
2. _____
3. _____
4. _____
5. _____
6. _____
7. _____
8. _____
9. _____
10. _____

Now go back and review each belief statement you wrote. Determine if the statement comes from an error consciousness or from Truth. For those that come from error, create a denial and a powerful affirmation you can use to expunge the error thought and implant Truth.

Your responses will vary, to reflect your own beliefs. A few examples would be:

1. I will never have enough money to do the things I would like to do. This would be a belief that comes from error consciousness.

   Denial: I give no power to the appearance of lack.

   Affirmation: I am the Divine flow of Abundance and have access to all the resources I ever need to do what is mine to do.

2. I give gladly, knowing my abundance is established in Oneness. This would be a belief grounded in Truth.

Chapter Thirty-Three—Creating a Metaphysical Demonstration Plan

The Heart of the Matter

List the six steps of creating a Metaphysical Demonstration Plan, as described in Chapter 33: Creating a Metaphysical Demonstration Plan.

Step 1: What is the situation, problem, challenge or need? (Describe)

Step 2: What do I hold in my mind that contributes to the situation, problem, challenge or need?

- How does this "serve" me?
- If there is another person involved, ask yourself: How is this person mirroring an aspect of myself?
- Am I resisting, and if so, how? Why?
- What am I feeling?
- What am I thinking?
- What am I sensing?
- What am I intuiting?
- What are my old mental messages or beliefs about this?
- Can I detect any other error thinking?

Step 3: What do I know about Oneness, my Christ Nature or Principle that can apply here?

Step 4: What Divine Ideas, Principles and Laws can I apply to this situation and how?

Step 5: What tools will help me with this situation?

- How am I going to apply them?
- When?
- How often?
- Where?
- Am I committed to doing this?

Step 6: Write a prayer of gratitude for the demonstration you are about to manifest, first in consciousness and then in form.

Putting It Into Practice

Using the material in Heart-Centered Metaphysics, *summarized in Chapter 33, create a Metaphysical Demonstration Plan of your own and put it into practice. For your first Metaphysical Demonstration Plan, choose something you have complete control over in your own consciousness. Don't try to swallow the big frog first. Start small and build your understanding, experience and confidence.*

Your Metaphysical Demonstration Plan will be unique to your specific needs. We have purposely not given you a concrete example because we feel the previous exercises have prepared you for this larger project. You may want to use the table that appears in Chapter 33 of *Heart-Centered Metaphysics* to help you.

Congratulations! We are proud of you for completing this workbook. Since you've gotten this far, we know you are on your way to fully being a Heart-Centered Metaphysician.

B0132